EARL
NIGHTINGALE
CLASSIC

LEAD
THE FIELD

AN OFFICIAL NIGHTINGALE CONANT PUBLICATION

SOUND WISDOM
P.O. Box 310
Shippensburg, PA 17257-0310

For more information on publishing and distribution rights, call 717-530-2122 or info@soundwisdom.com.

Quantity Sales. Special discounts are available on quantity purchases by corporations, associations, and others. For details, contact the Sales Department at Sound Wisdom.

ISBN13 HC: 978-1-64095-038-2
ISBN 13 TP: 978-1-64095-042-9
ISBN 13 Ebook: 978-1-64095-039-9

Lead the Field is a registered trademark of Nightingale-Conant Corporation.

For Worldwide Distribution, Printed in the U.S.A.
1 2 3 4 5 6 7 8 / 18 17 16 15

Cover design by Eileen Rockwell
Interior design by Susan Ramundo

CONTENTS

Introduction   7

1   **The Magic Word**   **9**
   Exercises   24

2   **Acres of Diamonds**   **27**
   Exercises   39

3   **A Worthy Destination**   **41**
   Exercises   57

4   **Miracle of Your Mind**   **59**
   Exercises   72

5   **Destiny in the Balance**   **75**
   Exercises   90

6   **Seed for Achievement**   **93**
   Exercises   104

7   **It's Easier to Win**   **107**
   Exercises   117

8   **How Much Are You Worth?**   **119**
    Exercises   130

9   **Let's Talk About Money**   **133**
    Exercises   145

10 **One Thing You Can't Hide**   **147**
    Exercises   159

11 **Today's Greatest Adventure**   **161**
    Exercises   171

12 **The Person on the White Horse**   **173**
    Exercises   184

INTRODUCTION

When was the last time something really excited you—excited you so much that you couldn't wait to share it with others? Often, such a reaction can be triggered by the simplest and most obvious things—such as a tiny puppy, or falling in love, or renewing an old friendship.

The great ideas in *Lead the Field* can have that effect on us, too. They can turn lives upside down. Suddenly, the lights are turned on, and we can see the world much more clearly. Opportunities take on a new luster, even though they have been there all the time, unnoticed, waiting for the great idea to make them all glow.

The multifaceted career of Earl Nightingale, author of *Lead the Field*, is an affirmation of the effect of great ideas on our lives and the degree of success we attain.

As a teenager, Earl saw the plight of his family and friends in the worst of the Depression. At that time, he couldn't afford any books. So he began seeking the answers, the keys to a better life, in his local library. And as a voracious reader, he kept searching throughout his life.

After serving in the U.S. Marines during World War II, Earl became a well-known broadcast personality and, over the years, authored more than 7,000 radio and television commentaries, as well as numerous audio and video programs and two best-selling books. For his many achievements as an entrepreneur, writer, public speaker, recording artist, and radio and television commentator, he won a number of awards, including a gold record for *The Strangest Secret* LP, for sales exceeding a million copies; the Golden Gavel Award from Toastmasters International; the Napoleon Hill Foundation Gold Medal Award for literary excellence; and he was inducted into the International Speakers Hall of Fame and the Radio Hall of Fame.

In *Lead the Field*, Earl Nightingale will lead you down new paths and old, familiar trails. You'll rediscover the power of words such as *attitude* and *service* and *goals* and *commitment*. You'll learn the use of "intelligent objectivity" and the benefit of being "constructively discontented." And with each repeated reading, you'll unearth new gems from these "acres of diamonds."

Over the years, hundreds of thousands of men and women have benefited from this treasury of great ideas. *Lead the Field* is the synthesis of a lifetime of research, reading, and refining by Earl Nightingale. Starting with your first chapter, "The Magic Word," the messages you're about to read are widely considered all-time classics in the field of personal development.

1

THE MAGIC WORD

This is Earl Nightingale with the new edition of *Lead the Field*. This book is about 12 ideas that will bring order and success into our lives. These ideas will work wonders, regardless of what we choose as the main thrust of our lives, for they are the great ideas that have evolved over the centuries, and together they form a constellation by which you and I can safely and successfully navigate.

The great Spanish philosopher, José Ortega y Gasset, reminded us that we human beings are born into a natural state of disorientation with our world. That is, while all other creatures are guided by instinct—of which they are unaware, and which they don't have the capacity to question—each of us, as a human creature, was given the godlike power to create his or her own life. And each of us does exactly that, all the years of his or her life. Every day, we put in place actions and ideas that will determine the shape and substance of our tomorrows. For some, those ideas and actions lead inevitably to extraordinary achievement and rewards. For most, they tend to lead to a kind of middle ground, in which great numbers of people take their cues from each other, without question or consideration. And for some, those actions and ideas lead to repeated frustration and problems, and they spend their lives in the bottom layers of the socioeconomic pyramid.

Success or failure as a human being is not a matter of luck, or circumstance, or fate, or the breaks, or who you know—or any of the other tiresome, old myths and clichés by which the ignorant tend to excuse themselves. It's a matter of following a common-sense paradigm of rules—guidelines anyone can follow.

Lead the Field has changed more lives, brought about more success stories, helped create more millionaires, and saved more careers, important jobs, and marriages than any other program ever produced. And the rules we talk about here don't change; they apply to any situation, under any and all circumstances. We never have to ask, "I wonder what will work in this particular situation?" All we have to do is make these ideas our own. And we begin with what I call "The Magic Word."

We all want good results from life, in our home, in our work, and in all our contacts with other people. The most important single factor that guarantees good results, day in, day out, all the months and years of our lives, is a healthy attitude! *Attitude* is the magic word.

Attitude is defined as "the position or bearing as indicating action, feeling, or mood." And it is our actions, feelings, or moods that determine the actions, feelings, or moods of others. Our attitude tells the world what we expect in return. If it's a cheerful, expectant attitude, it says to everyone with whom we come in contact that we expect the best in our dealings with our world.

You see, we tend to live up to our expectations. And others give to us, as far as their attitudes are concerned, what we expect. Our attitude is something we can control. We can establish our attitude each morning when we start our day—in fact, we do just that, whether or not we realize it. And the people in our family— all the people in our world—will reflect back to us the attitude we present to them.

It is, then, our attitude toward life that determines life's attitude toward us. Cause and effect. Everything we say or do will cause a corresponding effect. If we're cheerful, glad to be experiencing this miracle of life, others will reflect that good cheer back to us. We are the kind of people others enjoy being around.

You and I are responsible for our lives. You and I produce causes all day long, every day of our lives. The environment can return to us only a corresponding effect. That's why I say that each of us determines the quality of his or her own life. We get back what we put out.

Here's a way to evaluate the quality of your attitude in the past: Would you say that people tend to react to you in a smiling, positive manner, giving you friendly greetings when you appear? Your answer to that question will tell the story.

I remember the time when a man and his wife bought a home across the street from me in Florida. The couple had moved to Florida from their home in Minnesota. They had planned the move for years. They were tired of the Northern winters, and he was an avid fisherman.

Several months passed, and one day, I was surprised to see them packing. I walked across the street and asked the man if they were leaving so soon after they had made the move. He nodded. "My wife hates it here," he said. "We're going back home." I asked him how in the world his wife could hate it here, what she didn't like about the place. After a few questions, the truth came out.

"She hasn't been accepted here," he said. "The other women of the community have left her strictly alone. She hasn't made any friends. She hasn't been asked to participate in any of the community activities."

"Has she let the other women know she's interested in participating in community activities?" I asked him.

He stopped what he was doing and looked at me. "No," he said. "No, she hasn't. She's been waiting for the women to ask her."

"And since she's stayed in the house, waiting for them to come to her, they've thought of her as a recluse, as a person who's not interested in making friends. So they've left her alone."

There was a long silence, and then he began nodding. "Yes, that's exactly what's happened," he said.

Yes, the women of the neighborhood should have come to her and introduced themselves, or invited her to a tea or luncheon, but they were reacting to her. She didn't know that the community could give her back only a reflection of her own attitude. Here was a woman in her 60s who had never learned the first important rule for successful living: that our surroundings will always reflect us; that our environment is a mirror—often a merciless mirror—of ourselves.

As soon as a person begins to change, his or her surroundings will change. And it works like this: great attitude, great results; good attitude, good results; fair or average attitude, fair or average results; poor attitude, poor results.

So each of us shapes his or her own life. And to an altogether unexpected extent, the shape and texture and the quality or lack of quality of our lives is determined by our habitual attitude. It sounds simple, doesn't it? But it's not quite that easy. For most of us, learning this new habit takes time. But once it becomes a habit-knit part of our lives, our world will change as dramatically as it would if we were walking from a dark cave into the bright light of day.

Most people never think about their attitudes at all. For most of them, it's a matter of beginning each day in neutral. Their attitudes are neither good nor bad; they are poised to react to whatever stimuli they encounter. If the stimulus is good, they will reflect it; if it's bad, they will reflect that, too. They are chameleons, going through their days reacting to whatever confronts them. And these are the people of our environment. That's why it's so important for us to control our attitudes, to make sure they're excellent or good.

A person with a poor attitude toward learning, for example, isn't going to learn very much. I know you can think of examples of this in your own life. Or if we take the attitude that we can't do something, we generally will not do it. With an attitude of failure, we're whipped before we start.

It was William James of Harvard University, the father of psychology in America, who said "Human beings can alter their lives by altering their attitudes of mind."

In trying to describe the attitude that has worked so well for me over the years, I found myself using two important words: *gratitude* and *expectant*. First, I'm grateful for the opportunity to live on this beautiful and astonishing planet Earth. In the morning, I wake up with a sense of gratitude. Second, I expect the best; I expect to reach the goals I establish for myself (we'll talk a good deal more about this concept later in the book). I find the idea of fulfilling those goals agreeable; hence, the attitude of expectancy. I know the world will give me back what I put out in the way of attitude, so it's up to me. I'm responsible.

There are millions of human beings who live narrow, darkened, frustrated lives—who live defensively—simply because they take a defensive, doubtful attitude toward themselves and, as a result, toward life in general. A person with a poor attitude becomes a magnet for unpleasant experiences. When those experiences come—as they must, because of his attitude—they tend to reinforce his poor attitude, thereby bringing more problems, and so on. The person becomes an example of self-generating, doom-fulfilling prophecy. And it's all a matter—believe it or not—of attitude. We get what we expect. Our outlook on life is a kind of paintbrush, and with it, we paint our world. It can be bright and filled with hope and satisfaction, or it can be dark and gloomy—lugubrious.

Sometimes, it's hard to convince people that the world they experience is a reflection of their attitude. They take the attitude that if only people would be nice to them, they would be nice in return. They're like the person sitting in front of the cold stove waiting for the heat. Until he puts in the fuel, there won't be any heat. It's up to him to act first. It has to start somewhere. Let it begin with us.

Attitude is the reflection of the person inside. Consider for a moment the people who go sailing through life, from one success to another, and who, when they occasionally fail at something, shrug it off and head right out again.

No matter what people do, wherever you find people doing an outstanding job and getting outstanding results, you'll find people with a good attitude. These people take the attitude that they can accomplish what they set out to accomplish. They take the attitude that *achievement is the natural order of things* (and it is). They take the attitude that there's no good reason on earth why they can't be as successful, as competent, as anyone else. They have a healthy attitude toward life and the things they want to accomplish. Because of that, they can accomplish some remarkable things. Others may call them successful, outstanding, brilliant, lucky, and so on. Quite frequently, they are no smarter or more talented than most other people, but they have the right attitude. They find their accomplishments not too difficult simply because it seems so few others are really trying or really believe in themselves. As to luck, forget it. Luck is what happens when preparedness meets opportunity, and opportunity is there all the time.

A person can be very efficient at his or her work, but if the corresponding excellent attitude isn't present, the person is a failure. A robot can do a great job, but only a human being can ennoble work with a great attitude and, by so doing, touch it with the magic of humanness—make it come alive and sing, make it truly worthwhile. That, my friend, makes the difference.

Successful people come in all sizes, shapes, ages, and colors, and they have widely varying degrees of intelligence and education. But they have one thing in common: They expect more good out of life than bad. They expect success more often than failure. And they do succeed.

There are things you want—worthwhile things. Take the attitude that there are a lot more reasons why you can reach those goals than fail in the attempt. Go after them, work at it, keep your attitude positive, cheerful, and expectant, and you'll get them. And as you do, you'll grow to reach new plateaus and be able to accomplish still more.

Remember this: Our environment, the world in which we live and work, is a mirror of our attitudes and expectations. If we feel that our environment could stand some improvement, we can bring about that change for the better by improving our attitude. The world plays no favorites. It's impersonal. It doesn't care who succeeds or who fails. Nor does it care if we change. Our attitude toward life doesn't affect the world and the people in it nearly as much as it affects us.

It would be impossible to even estimate the number of jobs that have been lost, promotions or good grades missed, sales lost, or marriages ruined by poor attitudes. But you can number in the millions the jobs that are held but hated, the marriages that are tolerated but unhappy, the parents and children who fail to understand and love one another—all because of people who are waiting for the world and others to change them. They don't understand that what they're getting is a reflection of themselves. Nothing can change until we do. When we change, our worlds will change. The answer is attitude!

How does one develop a good attitude? The same way one develops any other ability: through practice! It's a good idea to stick on the bathroom mirror a small sign on which is printed the word *attitude!* That way, you'll see it first thing every morning. You might have another sign in your car and one at your place of work. We need to smile more, speak to people, go out to people.

Everything in the world we want to do or get done, we must do with and through people. Every dollar we will ever earn must come from people. The person we love, and with whom we want to spend the rest of our life, is a human being with whom we must interact. Our children are individuals, each different from any other person who ever lived. And what affects them most is our attitude—the loving-kindness they see and feel whenever we are around them.

If you'll begin to develop and maintain an attitude that says yes to life and the world, you'll be astonished at the changes you'll see.

Someone once said, "Life is dull only to dull people." It's true, of course. It's true also that life is interesting only to interesting people, and that life is successful only for successful people. We must be the epitome—the embodiment—of success. We must radiate success before it will come to us. We must first become mentally, from the attitude standpoint, the people we wish to become.

Many years ago, a newspaper reporter asked a famous Los Angeles restaurateur, "When did you become successful?"

He replied, "I was successful when I was dead broke. I knew what I wanted to do, and I knew I'd do it. It was only a matter of time."

He had a successful attitude long before the success he sought had become a reality.

The great German philosopher and writer, Goethe, put it this way: "Before you can do something, you must be something."

But let me prove my point by giving you an exercise. If you will conscientiously go about the exercise I will outline, and concentrate on it every day, you will find yourself becoming "lucky," as the uninitiated call it. All sorts of wonderful things will begin happening in your life, and it will show you what a great attitude can mean. So here's the exercise: Treat every person with whom you come in contact as the most important person on earth. Do that for three excellent reasons: (1) As far as every person is concerned, he is the most important person on earth. (2) That is the way human beings ought to treat each other. And (3) by treating everyone this way, we begin to form an important habit.

There's nothing in the world that men, women, and children want and need more than self-esteem—the feeling that they're important, that they're recognized, that they're needed, that they count and are respected. They will give their love, their respect, and their business to the person who fills this need.

Have you ever noticed that the higher you go in any organization of value, the nicer the people seem to be? It works this way: The bigger the people, the easier it is to talk to them, get along with them, and work with them. So they naturally matriculate to the top. It's their attitude. The people with great attitudes just naturally gravitate to the top of whatever business or department they're in. They don't have great attitudes because of their positions; they have their positions largely because of their great attitudes.

For the purposes of this exercise, act toward others in exactly the same manner that you want them to act toward you. Treat the members of your family as the very important people they are, the most important in the world. Each morning, carry out into the world the kind of attitude you'd have if you were the most successful person on earth. Notice how quickly it develops into a habit. Almost immediately, you'll notice a change. Irritations that used to frustrate you will begin to disappear. When some less-informed person gives you a bad time, don't let his poor attitude infect yours. Keep yours in hand; keep it good; keep cool, above it all; and keep smiling. If you're driving and someone cuts in front of your car, or if someone is discourteous to you in any other manner, don't react as he would; smile it off.

Destructive emotions, such as anger, hatred, and jealousy don't hurt others; they hurt you. They can make your life miserable. They can make you sick. Forgive everyone who ever hurt you—really forgive them—and then forgive yourself. That's all past. Stewing over it, exhuming it, can only make you sick. Forgive and forget. Get rid of it. You've risen above that sort of thing.

As you develop a great attitude, you'll probably realize that you've already placed yourself on the road to what you seek. You are well on your way. It makes no difference how successful you may have been in the past. You'll be delighted with the ease and comfort of your new life.

The bad or poor attitudes of others can be as infectious as the common cold. It's important that we look on them in this light: as infectious conditions that can end up only hurting and annoying

THE MAGIC WORD • 21

us if we allow ourselves to catch them. Like the doctor who often treats people with infectious conditions, we must keep ourselves healthy. We simply can't take time for that sort of thing.

Whoever coined the cliché "Life's too short" certainly knew what he was talking about. It really is too short—much too short—to spend any of our valuable time mimicking the attitudes of others—unless their attitudes are good.

A great attitude does much more than turn on the lights in our worlds; it seems to magically connect us to all sorts of serendipitous opportunities that were somehow absent before the change. Maybe that's what people mean when they say we're lucky. Suddenly, we do find ourselves getting the so-called "breaks." But it's really nothing more than this new connection to the world that comes with a great attitude. We find ourselves doing more and doing it in less time. We put ourselves directly in the path of all kinds of serendipitous happenings.

When you begin to develop a better attitude, you should realize that you've already placed yourself among the top 5 percent of the people—among the most successful people on earth. You've placed yourself on the road to what you seek. You've prepared the ground; you've only to plant the seed.

Now, in summing up, here are a few points to keep in mind:

First, it's our attitude at the beginning of a difficult task which, more than anything else, will bring about its successful outcome.

Secondly, our attitudes toward others determine their attitudes toward us. We're all interdependent. The success we achieve in life will depend largely on how well we relate to others.

Thirdly, before you can achieve the kind of life you want, you must think, act, talk, and conduct yourself in all of your affairs as would the person you wish to become. Keep a mental picture of that person before you as often as you can during the day.

Fourthly, remember that the higher you go in any organization of value, the better the attitudes you'll find. And that great attitudes are not the result of success; success is the result of great attitudes.

Finally, the deepest craving of the human being is for recognition and self-esteem—to be needed, to feel important, to be recognized and appreciated. That includes our loved ones and everyone else with whom we come in contact during our days.

To make these important principles a habit-knit part of your life, here are some suggestions:

Since your mind can hold only one thought at a time, make each thought you hold constructive and positive. Look for the best in people and ideas. Be constantly alert for new ideas you can put to use in your life.

Don't waste time talking about your problems with people who can't solve them, or about your health unless it's good or you're talking to your doctor. It won't help you. It can't help others.

Radiate the attitude of well-being and confidence, the attitude of the person who knows where he or she is going. You'll find all sorts of good things happening to you.

Lastly, treat everyone with whom you come in contact as the most important person on earth. Start this habit, practice it consistently, and you'll do it—and benefit from it—for the rest of your life.

Thank you.

EXERCISES

1. Evaluate your attitude toward yourself and others, toward success and your career, and toward life in general.

   _____

   _____

   _____

   _____

   _____

   _____

   _____

   _____

   _____

   _____

2. Outline ways in which your attitude toward your family could be improved.

   _____

   _____

   _____

   _____

   _____

   _____

   _____

   _____

   _____

   _____

3. Outline ways in which your attitude toward coworkers and others with whom you frequently come in contact could be improved.

_____

_____

_____

_____

_____

_____

_____

_____

_____

4. List other attitude-improvement goals.

_____

_____

_____

_____

_____

_____

_____

_____

_____

2

ACRES OF DIAMONDS

In 1843, a man was born who was to have a profound effect upon the lives of millions of people. His name was Russell Herman Conwell. He became a lawyer, then a newspaper editor, and, finally, a clergyman. During his church career, an incident occurred that was to change his life and the lives of countless others.

One day, a group of young people came to Dr. Conwell at his church and asked him if he would be willing to instruct them in college courses. They all wanted a college education but lacked the money to pay for it. He told them to let him think about it and to come back in a few days.

After they left, an idea began to form in Dr. Conwell's mind. He asked himself, "Why couldn't there be a fine college for poor but deserving young people?" Before very long, the idea consumed him. Why not, indeed? It was a project worthy of 100 percent dedication—complete commitment.

Almost singlehandedly, Dr. Conwell raised several million dollars with which he founded Temple University, today one of the country's leading schools. He raised the money by giving more than 6,000 lectures all over the country, and in each one of them, he told a story called "Acres of Diamonds." It was a true story that had affected him very deeply, and it had the same effect on his audiences. The money he needed to build the college came pouring in.

The story was the account of an African farmer who had heard tales about the other farmers who had made millions by discovering diamond mines. These tales so excited the farmer that he could hardly wait to sell his farm and go prospecting for diamonds himself. So he sold the farm and spent the rest of his life wandering the African continent, searching unsuccessfully for the gleaming gems that brought such high prices on the markets of the world. Finally, the story goes, worn out and in a fit of despondency, he threw himself into a river and drowned.

Meanwhile, back at the ranch, or farm, in this case, the man who had bought the farm happened to be crossing the small stream on the property. Suddenly, there was a bright flash of blue and red light from the stream's bottom. He bent down, picked up the stone—it was a good-sized stone—and, admiring it, later put it on his fireplace mantel as an interesting curiosity.

Several weeks later, a visitor to his home picked up the stone, looked closely at it, hefted it in his hand—and nearly fainted. He asked the farmer if he knew what he'd found. When the farmer said no, that he'd thought it was a piece of crystal, the visitor told him he'd found one of the largest diamonds ever discovered. The farmer had trouble believing that. He told the man that his creek was full of such stones—not as large, perhaps, as the one on the mantel, but they were sprinkled generously throughout the creek bottom.

Needless to say, the farm the first farmer had sold so that he might find a diamond mine turned out to be the most productive diamond mine on the entire African continent. The first farmer had owned, free and clear, acres of diamonds, but he had sold them for practically nothing in order to look for them elsewhere.

The moral is clear: If only the first farmer had taken the time to study and prepare himself—to learn what diamonds looked like in their rough state—and, since he had already owned a piece of the African continent, to thoroughly explore the property he had before looking elsewhere, all of his wildest dreams would have come true.

The thing about this story that so profoundly affected Dr. Conwell, and subsequently, millions of others, was the idea that each of us is, at this moment, standing in the middle of his or her own acres of diamonds.

If only we will have the wisdom and patience to intelligently and effectively explore the work in which we are now engaged, to explore ourselves, we'll usually find the riches we seek, whether they be financial or intangible, or both. Before we go running off to what we think are greener pastures, let's make sure that our own is not just as green or, perhaps, even greener. It's been said that if the other guy's pasture appears to be greener than ours, it's quite possible that it's getting better care. Besides, while we're looking at other pastures, other people are looking at ours!

To my mind, there are few things more pitiful than the person who wastes his life running from one thing to another, forever looking for the pot of gold at the end of the rainbow and never staying with one thing long enough to find it.

No matter what your goal may be, perhaps the road to it can be found in the very thing you're now doing. It wasn't until he was completely paralyzed by polio, and forced to reach into the rich resources of his mind, that a courageous farmer got the idea of producing exceptionally good meat products on his farm. From that idea, one of the country's most successful meat-packing companies was born. His farm contained acres of diamonds, too. He'd just never been forced to dig for them before.

Your mind is your richest resource. Let it thoroughly explore the possibilities lurking in what you're presently doing before turning to something new. I say that because there were probably good reasons for your having chosen your present work in the beginning. If there weren't, and if you're unhappy in the field you're in, then perhaps it's time for some serious exploration.

Dr. Russell Conwell's life is an example of the importance of a willingness to change once one's own pasture has been thoroughly explored. As I mentioned earlier, Dr. Conwell began as a lawyer, then became a newspaper editor before he finally found his true calling as a clergyman and the founder of a great university.

One of the best examples of a person's finding acres of diamonds hiding in his work is the story of Stew Leonard of Norwalk, Connecticut. Stew Leonard began as a dairy-route deliveryman. As he worked his rounds, he began to think of all the products connected to the dairy business that his customers really needed. With very little down, he bought a working dairy, and with a lot of hard work, he began to build a business around it. He kept the working dairy intact and the center of his operations, and he surrounded it with windows through which his customers could watch the process. And he began to add other products to his line.

Today, his dairy store is the largest in the world, and he sells everything in the food line. People come from all over the area to shop at Stew Leonard's World's Largest Dairy Store. They love it, and he loves them. People who are too old or infirm to come to his store on their own are picked up in Stew Leonard's buses and brought to the store. He has a multimillion-dollar business that grew out of a delivery route. The diamonds were there, and Stew Leonard made the most of them.

Every kind of work has such opportunity lurking within it. The opportunities are there now, clamoring to be noticed. But they cannot speak, or print signs for us to read. Our part of the bargain is to look at our work with new eyes, with the eyes of creation.

Pierre Teilhard de Chardin said, "It is our duty as men and women to proceed as though limits to our abilities do not exist. We are collaborators in creation."

A man I knew in Arizona began with a small gas station. One day, he was sitting at his desk and watching through the window while one of his young attendants filled a customer's gas tank. He watched the customer while he stood about, waiting for the job to be finished. It dawned upon him that that man had money in his pockets and that there were things he needed, or wanted, that he would pay for, if they were conveniently displayed where he could see them. So he began selling other items: fishing tackle, then fishing licenses, hunting and camping equipment, rifles, shotguns, ammunition, hunting licenses. He found an excellent line of aluminum fishing boats and trailers. He began buying up the contiguous property around him. Then he added an auto-parts department. He had always carried cold soft drinks and candy, but now he added an excellent line of chocolates in a refrigerated case. Before long, he sold more chocolates than anyone else in the state. He carried thousands of things his customers could buy while they waited for their cars to be serviced. All of this guaranteed that most of the gas customers in town would come to his station. He sold more gas. He began cashing checks on Fridays. The bonanza grew and grew.

It all started with a man with a human brain, watching a customer who was standing around with money in his pockets and nothing to spend it on. Others would have lived and died with the small service station—and they do. My friend saw the diamonds.

Both my friend in Arizona and Stew Leonard in Connecticut are customer-oriented. Serve the customer; serve the customer better than anyone else is serving the customer. Stew Leonard's company policy is conspicuously displayed in his store for all to read, and it goes like this: "Rule 1. The customer is always right! Rule 2. If the customer is ever wrong, reread Rule 1."

Upon seeing a wealthy customer drive in, many service-station operators might say to themselves, "I ought to be in his business." Not so. There is just as much opportunity in one business as there is in another, if only we will stop playing copycat with each other and begin thinking creatively—begin thinking in new directions. It's there, believe me. And it's our job to find it.

Take the time to stand back and look at your work as a stranger might. A stranger might ask, "Why does he do it that way? Has he noticed how what he's doing might be capitalized upon—or multiplied?"

If you're happy with things as they are, then, by all means, keep them that way. But there's great fun in finding diamonds hiding in ourselves and in our work. We never get bored or blasé, or find ourselves in a rut. (A rut, we're reminded, is really nothing more than a grave with the ends kicked out.) Some of the most interesting businesses in the world grew out of what was originally a very small idea in a very small area. If something is needed in one town, then the chances are that it's needed also in all towns and cities all over the country.

You might ask yourself also, "How good am I at what I'm presently doing?" Do you know all there is to know about your work? Would you call yourself a first-class professional at your work? How would your work stand up against the work of others in your line?

The educator and author J.B. Mathews wrote: "Unless a person has trained himself for this chance, the chance will only make him ridiculous. A great occasion is worth to a man exactly what his preparation enables him to make of it." (I'm sure Dr. Mathews intended to include the female half of the world in that statement.)

I'm often appalled by how little people know about the business they're in. "That's not my department," they'll say. (I suppose if they would see a fire starting in someone else's department, they wouldn't report it.) Most real-estate people don't sell homes and property. They *show* homes and property—something a six-year-old child could do. They often know nothing at all about selling or marketing, yet they call themselves real-estate professionals. They're actually tour guides. "This is the living room," they say to intelligent men and women who already know what a living room looks like.

Someone (come to think of it, I think it was I) once wrote that the human race is much like a convoy of ships in time of war; the whole fleet is slowed down to protect the slowest ships.

And human beings march slowly en masse, unmindful of the diamonds beneath their feet. To become diamond miners, the first thing we need to do is to break away from the crowd, and quit assuming that because people in the millions are living that way, it must be the best way. It's not the best way; it's the average way. The people going the best way are way out in front. They're so far ahead of the crowd, you can't even see their dust anymore. They're the people who live and work on the leading edge, the cutting edge. And they mark the way for all the rest.

You and I have a choice to make, really. It takes imagination, curious imagination, to see diamonds in their rough state as cut and polished gemstones, and to see a pile of iron ore as stainless steel.

To prospect for your own acres of diamonds, develop a faculty we might call "intelligent objectivity"—the faculty to stand back and look at your work as a person from Mars might look at it. Within the framework of what industry or profession does your job fall? Do you know all you can know about your industry or profession? Isn't it time for a refreshing change of some kind? How can the customer be given a better break?

Each morning, ask yourself: How can I increase my service today? There are rare and very marketable diamonds lurking all around me; have I been looking for them, examining every facet of my work and of the industry or profession in which it has its life? There are better ways to do what I'm presently doing; what are they? How will my work be performed 20 years from now? Everything in the world is in a state of evolution; how can I do now what will eventually be done anyway?

Think of what Stew Leonard did with his dairy route, and my friend in Arizona, with his small service station—what "Famous" Amos did with his chocolate-chip cookies, and what Procter and Gamble did with soap. Sure there's risk involved. There's no growth of any kind without risk. We start running risks when we get out of bed in the morning. Risks are good for us. They bring out the best that's in us. They brighten the eye and get the mind cooking. They quicken the step and put a new, shining look on our days.

Human beings should never be settled. It's OK for chickens and cows and cats, but it's wrong for human beings. People start to die when they become settled. We need to keep things stirred up.

Back in 1931, Lloyd C. Douglas, the world-famous novelist who wrote *The Robe, Magnificent Obsession* and other best-selling books, wrote a magazine article titled "Escape." In that article, Douglas asked, "Who of us has not at some time toyed briefly with the temptation to run away? If all the people who have given that idea the temporary hospitality of their imagination were to have acted upon it, few would be living at their present address. And of the small minority who did carry the impulse into effect, it is doubtful if many ever disengaged themselves as completely as they had hoped from the problems that hurled them forth. More often that otherwise, it may be surmised, they packed up their troubles in their old kit bags and took them along."

The point of the article was, simply, don't try to run away from your troubles. Overcome them; prevail, right where you are.

What we're really after is not escape from our perplexities and frustrations, but a triumph over them. And one of the best ways to accomplish that is to get on course and stay there.

Restate and reaffirm your goal—the thing you want most to do, the place in life you want most to reach. See it clearly in your mind's eye, just as you can envision the airport in Los Angeles when you board your plane in New York. Or, like a great ship in a storm, just keep your heading and your engines running. The storm will pass, although sometimes it seems that it never will, and one bright morning, you'll find yourself passing the harbor light. Then you can give a big sigh of relief, rest a while, and almost before you know it, you'll find your eyes turning seaward again. You'll think of a new harbor you'd like to visit—a new voyage upon which to embark—and once again, you'll set out.

That's just the way this funny-looking, two-legged, curious, imaginative, tinkering, fiddling dreamer called a human being operates. He escapes from problems not by running away from them but by overcoming them. And as soon as he overcomes one set of problems, he starts looking around for new and more difficult pickles to get himself into—and out of.

So if you find yourself looking at travel folders and thinking of running away, go ahead—think about it. It will get your mind off things for a while. Then zero in on your goal (we'll talk more about that later in this book), and get busy. Take one thing at a time, and before you know it, you'll start seeing those diamonds scattered all over your world, and you'll be out in the clear again.

If you feel like running away from it all once in a while, you're perfectly normal. If you stay and get rid of your problems by working your way through them, you're a successful citizen. Start taking an hour a day with a legal pad and pen to dissect your work. Take it apart and look at its constituent parts. There's opportunity there—that's your acre of diamonds.

EXERCISES

1. List opportunities that surround you now, in your current
    work. Brainstorm; write down whatever comes to mind.

    _____

    _____

    _____

    _____

    _____

    _____

    _____

    _____

    _____

2. How can you increase your knowledge of your current job,
    trade, industry or profession?

    _____

    _____

    _____

    _____

    _____

    _____

    _____

    _____

    _____

3. How can you improve your job performance now?

_____

_____

_____

_____

_____

_____

_____

_____

_____

3

A WORTHY DESTINATION

The stories of people achieving unusual success despite all manner of handicaps never fail to capture our attention. They're inspirational, to be sure. But if we study them closely, we find they're much more than that.

The boy whose legs were terribly burned and who was told he'd be lucky to walk again becomes a champion track star. The woman who was blind and deaf from early childhood becomes one of the most inspirational figures of the century. And the poor children who rise to fame and fortune have nearly become commonplace.

In this age of unprecedented immigration, we read and see on television examples of people who arrived in this country without any money and without knowing a word of English and who, within a surprisingly short time, have become wonderfully successful. In fact, the typical Korean family that has immigrated to the United States during the past 20 years has a higher average income than the average American family that was born and went to school here. How does that happen?

Freedom, personal liberty, is the most precious thing on earth. It's also one of the rarest—hence, its great value. People who manage to get to America, despite mountainous problems and miles of red tape, often find themselves free for the first time in their lives. It's a joyous, wonderful experience for them. And in this new-found freedom, they set to work to find a place for themselves; they go to work serving their new country and its people. Time means nothing to them. But being free to pursue their own ends in the richest, freest country on the planet is everything. They all go to work, and they work hard. Their work is excellent, first-class, as good as they can do it, and it's priced fairly. You don't see them marching, demanding higher pay or shorter hours. All they want is the opportunity, and once it's theirs, they make the most of it.

In New York City, a Korean family managed to buy a small convenience grocery store in midtown Manhattan. The first thing they did was clean it. The store sparkled with cleanliness. Then they stocked it with all the grocery items they felt the people in their area wanted. They were open early in the morning. They stayed open late at night. They never failed to give a friendly greeting to their customers. Naturally, they became wonderfully successful.

They were open seven days a week. One day, customers coming to the store found it closed. On the door was a note explaining the reason why. It read, "We have gone to Yale University to watch our son graduate."

That's an American story, the true story of people who found joy in freedom and in the opportunity to serve their fellow man— and who made the most of it.

What drives these people with such vast handicaps, such as not knowing the language, not knowing the right people, not having any money? Or the boy with the burned legs who becomes the champion runner? Or a Helen Keller, blind and deaf from early childhood? What in the world is the answer?

The answer, if fully understood, will bring you and me anything and everything we truly want. And it's deceptively simple. We touched on it in our last chapter. Perhaps it's too simple.

The people we have talked about here, and the thousands currently doing the same thing all over the country, possess something the average American doesn't have: They have *goals*. They have a burning desire to succeed despite all handicaps. They know exactly what they want. They think about it every day of their lives. It gets them up in the morning, and it keeps them giving their very best all day long. It's the last thing they think about before dropping off to sleep at night. They have a vision of exactly what they want to do, and that vision carries them over every obstacle.

This vision, this dream, this goal—invisible to all the world except the person holding it—is responsible for perhaps every great advance and achievement of humankind. It's the underlying motive for just about everything we see about us. Everything worthwhile that has been achieved by men and women is a dream come true, a goal reached.

It's been said that what the mind can conceive and believe, it can achieve. It's the fine building where before there was an empty lot or an ancient eyesore. It's the bridge spanning the bay. It's landing on the moon. It's that little convenience store in midtown Manhattan. It's the lovely home on a tree-shaded street, and the young person accepting the diploma. It's the new baby in its mother's arms. It's a low golf handicap, and a position reached in the world of business. It's a certain income attained or amount of money invested. What the mind can conceive and believe, it can achieve.

We become what we think about. And when we're possessed by an exciting goal, we reach it. That's why it's been said, "Be choosy, therefore, what you set your heart upon. For if you want it strongly enough, you'll get it." Amen to that.

It's been said that Americans can have anything they want; the trouble is that they don't know what they want. Oh, they want little things. They want a new car, and they get it. They want a new home, and they get it. The system never fails to work for them. But they don't seem to understand that it is a system, and that if it will work for a new refrigerator or a new car, it will work just as well for anything else they want very much. . . .

Once a person fully understands that the goals that are important to him can become real in his life, well, it's like opening a jack-in-the-box: All sorts of interesting and exciting things begin to happen. Quite often, we become truly alive for the first time in our lives. We look back at our former lives and realize we were shuffling along in a kind of lockstep; that we were actually taking our cues from those about us, in the unspoken assumption that we're all alike, when nothing could be farther from the truth. We are not all alike. Each of us is quite different, with different abilities, different genetic profiles, different wants in life. What would wonderfully satisfy one family, and represent complete success for them, would be considered failure by another family—all because of their different aspirations, their different plateaus in life, the differences in their lifestyles, upbringings, educations.

When we're youngsters, every facet of our environment has an effect upon us and helps to set our course in life. The youngster who knew poverty as a child might aspire to be rich—he might overcompensate because of the desolation of his youth—while another young person, who was raised in an upper-middle-class family and who always had just about everything he wanted, might settle for a very middle-class adulthood. Things we've always had aren't as important to us as they are to those who have been without them.

In the preceding chapter, we talked about freedom and about how dear it is to those who never had it, while most Americans take it for granted and never even think about it. If you asked most Americans what the most important thing in the world is for a human being, chances are they would seldom come up with freedom—the freedom to set their own goals in life. Yet, as Archibald MacLeish wrote in his fine play *The Secret of Freedom*, "The secret of happiness is freedom; and the secret of freedom, courage."

To understand the subject, and the importance of goal setting, we have to realize that it is the very basis of any success. It is, in fact, the very definition of success.

The best definition of success I've ever found goes like this: "Success is the progressive realization of a worthy goal," or, in some cases, ". . . the pursuit of a worthy ideal."

If you'll give this definition some thought, I think you'll agree with me: Success is the progressive realization of a worthy goal. That's a beautiful definition of success. It means that anyone who's on course toward the fulfillment of a goal is successful now. Success does not lie in the achievement of a goal, although that's what the world considers success; it lies in the journey toward the goal. We're successful as long as we're working toward something we want to bring about in our lives. That's when the human being is at his best. That's what Cervantes meant when he wrote, "The road is better than the inn."

Quite often, romantic stories end with the loving couple getting married. That's just the beginning of the story. When the young person stands before his school's president or principal and receives the diploma, that's called commencement. That's the beginning. It's an important milestone, to be sure, and congratulations are certainly in order. But where is he going from there?

Once a person has realized the goal for which he has so assiduously toiled, that's wonderful. It's time for a rest and some self-congratulations—time to savor the achievement. But by my definition, we're no longer successful until we set a new, higher goal toward which to work. We're at our best when we're climbing, thinking, planning, working—when we're on the road to something we want to bring about.

By this, I don't mean that we should become workaholics—far from it. In fact, it's been well-established that the most successful men and women manage to live in a wonderful state of balance. They have lots of recreation, and they get lots of rest. The mind works best when we're properly rested, and the mind is the best and most important part of us, regardless of what we choose to do.

Have you heard an athlete say, "It's about 90 percent mental"? Whatever the percentage really is in a good game of golf or tennis, it's very large. As we pointed out in Chapter 1, "The Magic Word," our mental attitude can make all the difference between winning and losing.

With our definition of success as the progressive realization of a worthy goal, we cover all the bases. The young person working to finish school is as successful as any person on earth. The person working toward a particular position with his company is just as successful.

If you have a goal that you find worthy of you as a person—a goal that fills you with joy at the thought of it—believe me, you'll reach it. But as you draw near and see that the goal will soon be achieved, begin to think ahead to the next goal you're going to set. It often happens that halfway through a book, a writer will hit upon the idea for his next one and begin making notes, or come up with ideas for a title—even while he's finishing work on the book in progress. That's the way it should be.

One of my favorite poems is by Rabindranath Tagore, the distinguished poet from Calcutta, India, and it goes like this: "I slept and dreamt / That life was joy / I woke and saw / That life was duty / I acted, and behold! / Duty was joy."

We are at our very best, and we are happiest, when we are fully engaged in work we enjoy on the journey toward the goal we've established for ourselves. It gives meaning to our time off and comfort to our sleep. It makes everything else in life so wonderful, so worthwhile.

When they think of the word *success*, most people tend to equate it with lots of money. Sometimes that's a natural by-product of the goal, and it tells us how well we're doing. But not always, by any means. Success is whatever we want it to be that's worthy of us. That's why I commented earlier that success may also be defined as the pursuit of a worthy ideal. For example, I can't imagine anyone more successful than an outstanding teacher who is striving to know more about the art of teaching and the subject matter that will catch the interest of his pupils, who understands that every student is different and learns at a different speed.

Joy and satisfaction come to us from serving others, and there are literally millions of ways of doing that. For those whose goals involve the serving of great numbers of people, chances are they will be richly rewarded, indeed. In fact, for many, a goal is a certain level of income, or a certain amount of money in an investment account.

A goal is an individual thing—as individual as the person himself. Since no two people are exactly alike, it stands to reason that no two of us will have exactly the same goals.

One thing a goal must do, however, is fill us with positive emotion when we think about it; it must be something we want very much to bring about. The more intensely we feel about an idea or a goal, the more assuredly the idea, buried deep in our subconscious, will direct us along the path to its fulfillment.

I once used the quotation, "No one gets rich without enriching others." I received a letter from a man in Utah who wrote: "How about those who get rich in the drug trade, or those who produce and sell pornography? How do they enrich others?"

It was a good question, especially in these times. I wrote back to him and told him that my definition of success is the progressive realization of a *worthy* goal. Certainly, people in the drug and pornography business would not qualify as successful. What they're doing is counterproductive, destructive. And in the case of drugs, it involves the enslavement and death of thousands.

I went on to say that while our needs are few, and relatively simple, our wants, in this incredibly affluent society, are virtually endless. By meeting those wants, whatever they may be, we serve others—but not always to their benefit or to our own. I wouldn't call those in drugs and pornography successful, and their riches won't amount to much if they're apprehended and sent to prison.

But I did not stop using the quotation. It's possible to get rich without enriching others, but for most of us, it's not the way we want to go. It's nothing to take pride in. Why bother when there are so many positive, excellent, and productive ways to serve others?

But whatever our goal happens to be, if we stay with it, if we're fully committed to it, we will reach it. That's the way it works.

It's estimated that about 5 percent of the population achieves unusual success. For the rest, averages seem to be good enough. Most seem to just drift along, taking circumstances as they come, and perhaps hoping from time to time that things will get better.

I like to compare human beings to ships, as Carlyle used to do. It's estimated that about 95 percent can be compared to ships without rudders. Subject to every shift of wind and tide, they're helplessly adrift. And while they fondly hope that they will one day drift into some rich and bustling port, you and I know that for every narrow harbor entrance, there are a thousand miles of rocky coastline. The chances of their drifting into port are a thousand to one against them.

Our state lotteries wax rich on such people. So do the slot machines in Las Vegas and Atlantic City. These people look to luck, but they don't seem to realize how steeply the odds are stacked against them. Someone wins from time to time, to be sure, but the odds are still there.

But the 5 percent who have taken the time and exercised the discipline to climb into the driver's seat of their lives, who have decided upon a challenging goal to reach and fully committed themselves to reaching it, sail straight and far across the deep oceans of life, reaching one port after another, and accomplishing more in just a few years than the rest accomplish in a lifetime.

If you should visit a ship in port and ask the captain for his next port of call, he'll tell you in a single sentence. Even though the captain cannot see his port, his destination, for fully 99 percent of the voyage, he knows that it's there, and that barring an unforeseen and highly unlikely catastrophe, he'll reach it. All he has to do is keep doing certain things every day.

If someone asked you for your next port of call, your current goal, could you tell him? Is your goal clear and concise in your mind? Have you written it down? It's a good idea. We need reminding, reinforcement. If you can get a picture of your goal and stick it to your bathroom mirror, it's an excellent idea to do so. Thousands of successful people write down their goal on a card and carry it in their wallet or purse.

When we ask people what they're working for, chances are they'll answer in vague generalities. They might say good health or happiness or lots of money. That's not good. Good health should be a universal goal; we all want that and do our best to achieve and maintain it. Happiness is a by-product of something else. And lots of money is much too vague. It might work, but I think it's better to choose a particular sum of money. The better, the more clearly, our goal is defined, the more real it becomes to us—and, before long, the more attainable.

Happiness comes from the direction in which we're moving. For example, children are happier on Christmas morning before they open their presents than they are on Christmas afternoon. No matter how wonderful their presents may be, the anticipation is over. They will enjoy their gifts, to be sure, but we often find them querulous and irritable on Christmas afternoon.

We are happier on our way out to dinner than we are on the way home. We are happier preparing to leave on vacation than we are coming home from it. And, believe it or not, we are happier moving toward our goals than we are after they've been accomplished. That's why it's so important to set a new goal as soon as the current one is realized. And we should never stop this process. All the days of our lives, we should be engaged in moving toward—earning and looking forward to—a new plateau on which to stand, a new goal to accomplish.

If you, like so many millions of Americans, don't know what it is you want sufficiently to name as your primary goal, I recommend you make out a "want list." Take a notepad, go off by yourself, and write down the things you would really like to have or to do. Your list might include a beautiful new home, or a trip around the world, or a visit to some special country or place. You might be yearning for a sailboat or a motor yacht. Or, if you're an avid fisherman, you might want to go salmon fishing in Alaska or trout fishing in New Zealand. It might be a business of your own, or a particular position with your company. It might be a certain income that will permit you to live in the way you would like to live, or, as I said earlier, a certain amount of money in good investments or in a savings account. How about a special make of car, or an addition to your present home?

Just write down everything you can think of that you would really like to see come about in your life. Then, when you've exhausted your wants, go over the list again and number the items in their order of importance. Then, make number one your present goal.

Reread this chapter often, as I hope you will read carefully all the chapters in this book, until the suggestions become a habit-knit way of thinking and doing things. Believe me, the system works. It works every time. Life plays no favorites. Anyone can succeed—and millions do. So can you.

Of one thing you can be sure: You will become what you think about. If your thinking is circular and chaotic, your life will reflect that chaos. But if your thinking is orderly and clear, if you have a goal that is important for you to reach, then reach it you will.

One goal at a time—that's important. That's where most people unwittingly make their mistake. They don't concentrate on a single goal long enough to reach it before they're off on another track, then another, with the result that they achieve nothing— nothing but confusion—and make excuses.

I started looking for the so-called secret of success when I was 12 years old. I read every book I could find on the subject; I studied psychology and sociology; I studied the great religions of the world; I read the world's greatest philosophers. All of a sudden, many years later, I realized that in the hundreds of lives I'd studied, in the countless books I'd read, a plain and simple truth had kept appearing. It is believed that no one can learn anything until he is ready for it. Apparently, I was finally ready, in my late 20s, to see for the first time the secret I had searched for so long. It was, simply this: We become what we think about.

You see, you are, at this moment, the living embodiment of the sum total of your thoughts to this point in your life. You can be nothing else. Similarly, five years from now, you will be the sum total of your thoughts to that point in time. But you can control your thoughts. You can decide upon what you wish to concentrate, upon what you think about from this point forward. And you will become that. You will realize that goal as sure as anything on earth can be sure. That's why having a goal toward which to work is so very important. It gives our minds a focus and our lives a direction.

By thinking every morning, every night, and as many times during the day as we can, about the single goal we've established for ourselves, we actually begin moving toward it, and bringing it toward us. When we concentrate our thinking, it's like taking a river that's twisting and turning and meandering all over the countryside, and putting it into a straight, smooth channel. Now it has power, direction, economy, speed.

Billions of human beings would give anything they have to enjoy the freedom and personal liberty you and I take for granted; to have the right to choose their work and their goals; to enjoy our bountiful standard of living and our educational system; to know the peace and privacy of our homes; and to have laws that protect the citizen rather than persecute him.

We have it all. Yet, in the midst of our plenty, millions lead unhappy, aimless lives, They live in tiny prisons of their own fashioning. These are the people who don't know that each of us—each one of us—not the economy or fate or luck or the breaks, is in charge of his life. Each one of us is completely responsible.

As Carlyle put it, "The person without a purpose is like a ship without a rudder. Have a purpose in life, and having it, throw such strength of mind and muscle into your work as God has given you."

He also said, "A person with a half-volition goes backward and forward, and makes no way on the smoothest road; but the person with a whole volition advances on the roughest, and will reach his purpose, if there be even a little wisdom in it."

Munger said, "There is no road to success but through a clear, strong purpose. Nothing can take its place. A purpose underlies character, culture, position, attainment of every sort."

So decide upon your goal. Insist upon it. Look at your goal card every morning and night and as many times during the day as you conveniently can. By so doing, you will insinuate your goal into your subconscious mind. See yourself as having already attained your goal. Do that every day without fail, and it will become a habit before you realize it—a habit that will take you from one success to another all the years of your life. For that is the secret of success, the door to everything you will ever have or be. You are now, and you most certainly will become, what you think about.

EXERCISES

1. Make out a want list—write down everything that you would like to see come about in your life.

_____

_____

_____

_____

_____

_____

_____

_____

_____

_____

_____

_____

_____

2. After you have completed your want list, number the items in their order of importance.

3. Make item number one your present primary goal; use the balance of the list for later reference.

4. Write down your current goal on a card, and carry it with you in your wallet or purse.

5. How will the achievement of this goal improve your life?

_____

_____

_____

_____

_____

_____

_____

_____

_____

_____

_____

_____

4

MIRACLE OF YOUR MIND

At birth, all creatures are supplied with everything they need for successful survival. All creatures except one are supplied with a set of instincts that will do the job for them, and because of that, they don't need much of a brain.

Take the magnificent bald eagle, for example. My wife and I saw dozens of bald eagles on a recent fishing trip to Alaska. To see one of them come swooping down and pluck a live and sizable fish from the water on a single pass is astonishing. More astonishing, still, is the eagle's eyesight. And because of its need to see from high altitudes small rodents moving in the grass, or a fish just inches under the surface of the water, its incredible eyes take up just about all the space in its head. For the eagle, its eyes are the most important thing, and everything else works in unison with them. Its brain is tiny and rudimentary. It doesn't think or plan or remember; it simply acts in accordance with stimuli.

It's the same with most other living creatures. Even the beautiful porpoise, which has a much larger brain, and the chimpanzee are easily tamed and taught.

Only one creature takes 20 years to mature, has dominion over all the rest and the earth itself, and has today the power to destroy all life on earth in a couple of hours. Only one creature is given the godlike power to fashion its own life according to the images it holds in its remarkable mind.

Everything fashioned by human beings is a result of goal setting. We reach our goals. That's how we know that the diseases that plague us will be conquered. We have set goals to eradicate all diseases that plague us—and eradicate them we will, one by one. We have never set a goal that we have not reached—even landing on the moon—or are not now in the process of reaching.

No one has ever made a purposeful accomplishment without a clear goal toward which to work. I hope you've established yours, and that you've begun to think about it frequently every day—to impress it into your mind, particularly your remarkable subconscious, where forces greater than we can imagine can come to your aid.

For a moment, consider the things your mind has brought you. Everything you have—your work, your relationships with your family and others, your philosophy of life, your religion—has come to you as a result of your using your mind. Now, consider this estimate made by experts: You have probably been operating on less than 10 percent of your mental capacity—and probably much less than that!

In an article for the *Saturday Review*, our old friend Herbert Otto, psychologist, educator, and chairman of the National

Center for the Exploration of Human Potential, reminded us that many well-known scientists, such as Abraham Maslow, Margaret Mead, Gardner Murphy, O. Spurgeon English, and Carl Rogers, subscribed to the hypothesis that man is using a very small fraction of his capacities. Margaret Mead quoted a 6 percent figure. Herbert Otto wrote, "My own estimate is 5 percent or less."

Neurological research has shed new light on man's potential. Work at the UCLA Brain Research Institute points to enormous abilities latent in everyone. Researchers there suggest an incredible hypothesis: The ultimate creative capacity of the human brain may be, for all practical purposes, *infinite*. To use the computer analogy, man is a vast storehouse of data, but we have not learned how to program ourselves to utilize these data for problem-solving purposes.

The following appeared in *Soviet Life Today*, a U.S.S.R. English-language magazine: "The latest findings in anthropology, psychology, logic, and physiology show that the potential of the human mind is very great indeed. As soon as modern science gave us some understanding of the structure and work of the human brain, we were struck with its enormous reserve capacity." That was written by Yefremov, an eminent Soviet scholar and writer. He continued: "Man, under average conditions of work and life, uses only a small part of his thinking equipment. . . . If we were able to force our brain to work at only half its capacity, we could, without any difficulty whatever, learn 40 languages, memorize the large Soviet encyclopedia from cover to cover, and complete the required courses of dozens of colleges."

That statement is hardly an exaggeration; it is the generally accepted theoretical view of man's mental potentials.

Now, how can we tap this gigantic potential? It's a big and very complex problem with many ramifications. But, as Herbert Otto pointed out, "It is clear that persons who live close to their capacity, who continue to activate their potential, have a pronounced sense of well-being and considerable energy. They see themselves as leading purposeful and creative lives."

The way most people use their minds can be compared to the time, back in the early 19th century, when just the Eastern coast of the North American continent was settled—just a strip along the East Coast. To the West stretched the raw, undeveloped, great bulk of what was later to become the incredibly rich 90 percent of the economy—90 percent of the natural resources—which resulted in the standard of living enjoyed today by Americans.

If everything you have is the result of your using just 5 or 10 percent of your mind, consider for a moment what it will mean to you and your family if you can increase this percentage! This program will show you how to use infinitely more of your mental powers, how to develop some of that 90 percent virgin territory.

None of us, as a rule, has the slightest notion of the real capabilities of his mind. But believe me when I say that your mind can be compared to an undiscovered gold mine. And it makes no difference whether you're 17 or 70.

Look at it this way: Your goal is in the future. Your problem is to bridge the gap that exists between where you now are and the goal you intend to reach. This is the problem to solve.

Robert Seashore, when he was chairman of the Department of Psychology at Northwestern University, pointed out that "Successful people are not people without problems; they're simply people who've learned to solve their problems."

There you have it. Living successfully, getting the things we want from life, is a matter of solving the problems that stand between where we are now and the point we wish to reach!

No one is without problems; problems are a part of living. But let me show you how much time we waste in worrying about the wrong problems. Here's a reliable estimate of the things people worry about: things that never happen, 40 percent; things over and past that can't be changed by all the worry in the world, 30 percent; needless worries about our health, 12 percent; petty miscellaneous worries, 10 percent; real, legitimate worries, 8 percent.

In short, 92 percent of the average person's worries take up valuable time, cause painful stress—even mental anguish—and are absolutely unnecessary.

Of the real, legitimate worries, there are two kinds: There are the problems we can solve, and there are the problems beyond our ability to personally solve. But most of our real problems usually fall into the first group: the ones we can solve, if we'll learn how.

There must be millions of people today who feel they are being barred from the life they want because they look upon problems not as challenges to be met, but as wide chasms beyond their ability to bridge.

A little research proves that successful people have the same kinds of problems other people have. One of the very real benefits of working with a psychologist or psychiatrist comes from learning that there are hundreds of thousands—perhaps millions—of other people with problems identical to our own. So the whole thing boils down to a matter not of problems, which are common to us all, but of our ability to solve them.

Now, I'm going to assume you have decided on a goal.

Remember, you will become, and you will achieve, what you think about. That is, if you stay with it, you will reach your goal. But how? Here is where your mind comes into play.

What is your mind, really? Perhaps the best way to describe it is to quote Pulitzer Prize-winning playwright Archibald MacLeish. In his play *The Secret of Freedom*, a character says, "The only thing about a man that is a man is his mind. Everything else you can find in a pig or a horse."

That's uncomfortably true. The human mind is the one thing that separates us from the rest of the creatures on earth. Everything that means anything to us comes to us through our minds. Our love of our families, our beliefs, all of our talents, knowledge, abilities—everything—is reflected through our minds. Anything that comes to us in the future will almost certainly come to us as a result of the extent to which we use our minds! And yet, it is the last place on earth the average person will turn to for help!

Do you know why? Do you know why most people don't automatically turn on their own vast mental resources when they're faced with a problem? It's because they've never learned how to think. That is a fact, believe it or not. Most people never think at all during the entire course of their lives. They remember, but that's not thinking creatively, or thinking in new directions. They react to stimuli, but again, that's not thinking. Remembering to set the alarm clock at night and getting up when it rings in the morning does not take thought. Nor do showering, shaving, getting dressed, eating breakfast, and going to work. At work, we once again fall into comfortable routines. At quitting time, we go home and start repeating the process.

Let me say it again: Most people do not know how to think. When they are faced with a problem, they will go to any length to avoid thinking. They will ask advice from the most illogical people—usually people who don't know any more than they do, such as next-door neighbors and members of their families. Very few of them have reference books. But much more important than that, only one in "I don't know how many thousands" will take a large notepad, write the problem at the top of the page, and then deliberately turn on his thinking apparatus.

But some people do think—they do, indeed. Reflect for a moment on the human mind; consider what it has accomplished!

As you do, realize that we are developing so rapidly that we've come farther in the realm of progress in the past 50 years than we have in all the preceding 10,000 years of human civilization.

Of all the scientists who ever lived, it's estimated that 90 percent of them are alive today!

In the area of ideas and human advancement, we've reached a plateau so high, it was undreamed of by even the most optimistic forecasters as recently as 30 years ago. But every new idea triggers additional ideas, so now we're in an era of compounding advancement in every area, and on every front, that staggers the imagination.

The harnessing of the power of the sun in our atomic plants and ships; the speed-of-light computers that, in minutes, save months and years of calculating drudgery—every advance you see and touch spawned from the most powerful agency in the world: the human mind.

Dr. Harlow Shapley of Harvard University said that we are entering an entirely new age of man. He called in the psychozoic age: the age of the mind. And you, my friend, own one! Free and clear!

Now, let's look at a few facts. The 40-hour week, long standard is in imminent likelihood of being shortened even further. This means that the average working person has, at his disposal, an enormous amount of free time. In fact, if you'll total the hours in a year and subtract the sleeping hours (assuming eight hours of sleep every night), you'll find that this person has about 6,000 waking hours, of which less than 2,000 are spent on the job. Now, this leaves 4,000 hours a year when a person is neither working nor sleeping. These can be called discretionary hours, with which that person can do pretty much as he pleases.

So you can see the amazing results in your life, I want to recommend that you devote just one hour a day, five days a week, to exercising your mind. You don't even have to do it on weekends. Pick one hour a day that you can count on fairly regularly. The best time for me is an hour before the others are up in the morning. The mind is clear, the house is quiet, and, if you like, with a fresh cup of coffee, this is the time to start the mind going.

And here's one good way to do this: During this hour every day, take a completely blank sheet of paper. At the top of the page, write your present primary goal—clearly and simply. Then, since our future depends upon the way in which we handle our work, write down as many ideas as you can for improving that which you do now. Try to think of 20 possible ways in which the activity that fills your day can be improved. You won't always get 20, but even one idea is good.

Now, remember two important points with regard to this: (1) This is not particularly easy, and (2) most of your ideas won't be any good.

When I say it's not easy, I mean it's like starting any other habit. At first, you'll find that your mind is a little reluctant to be hauled up and out of the old, familiar rut. But as you think about your work and ways in which it might be improved, write down every idea that pops into your head, no matter how absurd it might seem.

Let me tell you what will happen. Some of your ideas will be good and worth testing. The most important thing this extra hour accomplishes, however, is that it deeply imbeds your goal into your subconscious mind and starts the whole vital machinery working, the first thing every morning. And 20 ideas a day, if you can come up with that many, total 100 a week, even if you skip weekends. An hour a day five days a week totals 260 hours a year and still leaves you 3,740 hours of free leisure time.

Now, this means you'll be thinking about your goal and ways of improving your performance—increasing your service—six-and-one-half full, extra working weeks a year! Six-and-one-half 40-hour weeks devoted to thinking and planning. Can you see how easy it is to rise above the so-called competition? And it will still leave you with seven hours a day to spend as you please!

Starting each day thinking, you will find that your mind will continue to work all day long. You will find that at odd moments, when you least expect it, really great ideas will begin to bubble up from your subconscious. When they do, write them down as you can. Just one great idea can completely revolutionize your work and, as a result, your life!

If you want to develop the muscles of your body, you engage in daily exercise of some sort. The mind is developed in the same way, except that the returns are out of all conceivable proportion to the time and energy spent. The mind of man can lift anything. His muscles—even the best developed—are puny alongside those of some of the dumbest animals on earth. If man had depended on his muscles for survival, he probably would have disappeared, as did the dinosaurs—which were, incidentally, the most physically powerful creatures that ever lived.

Let me give you just some of the results people have reported to me as a consequence of following this one-hour-a-day routine: An office-equipment salesman sold more of his company's product in one month than he had formerly sold in an entire year during the four years he had been with his company. And a Sunday-school teacher with five pupils set a goal of 30 pupils. In her last letter, she told me she now has a class of 25. She's almost reached her goal.

I've used this system for years, and it has given me some of the most gratifying and rewarding experiences of my life. And it costs only five hours per week—five hours out of 168. Is it worth it? It's like spending five hours a week digging in a solid vein of pure gold, because your mind is all of that—and much more!

Each time you write your goal at the top of a sheet of paper, don't worry or become concerned about it. Think of it as only waiting to be reached, a problem only waiting to be solved. Face it with faith, and bend all the great powers of your mind toward solving it, and, believe me, solve it you will!

This puts each of us in the driver's seat.

Now, let's briefly recap:

This week, start spending one hour each day getting as many ideas as you can—try for 20 a day—on ways to improve what you are now doing. Don't become discouraged. Remember, the achievement of your goal very likely depends upon it, as does your whole future. Once you start exercising your mind in this way, I know you'll want to continue the practice.

If everything you now have is the result of using, say, 5 to 10 percent of your mental ability, you can imagine what life will be like if you can increase this figure to 20 percent or more.

Successful people are not people without problems; they are simply people who have learned to solve their problems.

Don't waste time and energy worrying about needless things. Forty percent of them will never happen; 30 percent have already happened and can't be changed; 12 percent are needless worries about our health; 10 percent are petty miscellaneous worries; and only 8 percent are genuine. Try to separate the real from the unnecessary, and solve those that are within your ability to solve.

The human race has advanced farther during the past 50 years than it has in all the preceding 10,000 years of human civilization. We are now living right in the middle of the golden age man has been dreaming of and praying for for centuries—and it's going to get better!

The only thing in the world that can take you to your goals in life is your mind, your effective use of it, and your follow-through on the good ideas it supplies you.

Each of us has a tendency to underestimate his own abilities. We should realize that we have, deep within ourselves, deep reservoirs of great ability—even genius—that can be tapped, if we'll just dig deeply enough. It's the "Miracle of Your Mind."

EXERCISES

1. List all your worries and concerns.

_____

_____

_____

_____

_____

_____

_____

_____

_____

_____

_____

_____

_____

_____

_____

_____

_____

_____

_____

_____

_____

2. From this list, determine which worries are needless and which are legitimate.

3. Outline a strategy for solving your legitimate problems.

_____

_____

_____

_____

_____

_____

_____

_____

_____

_____

_____

_____

_____

_____

_____

_____

_____

4. Starting this week, spend one hour each day exercising your mind. That is, write down ideas for improving your present and/or achieving your current goal. Strive for 20 ideas each day.

5. Test the ideas that you believe have merit.

5

DESTINY IN THE BALANCE

I'm sure you find it as amazing as do the rest of us that the great majority of people have to learn things the hard way. It's only natural to think that if a great discovery were made in a particular generation, all the succeeding generations would know about it and utilize it for their own good. But in many things, such is not the case.

It's true with most inventions and discoveries that obviously affect our lives, but it frequently is not true when it comes to the great laws that determine the direction of our individual destinies.

In one of the Third World countries, a group of laborers was hired to work on a farm. These people came from a small, very remote village where motor vehicles were virtually unknown. They were enjoying the new experience of being transported on the back of a truck when they came to the place where they thought they were supposed to get off. Without giving it a thought, apparently, they just stepped off the back of the speeding truck.

Fortunately, they fell on a soft, dirt road—not a paved highway. But even so, the results of their unconventional method of disembarking were, to say the least, astonishing—at least to them. They went bounding, spinning, sliding and cartwheeling along the dusty road for quite a distance until gravity and friction, working together, finally brought them to a halt. None was seriously injured. In fact, by the time the terrified driver got back to them, they were laughing uproariously about the whole thing.

In explaining the incident later, the truck driver put the blame on their never having ridden in a truck before. That's the obvious answer, but it's really not the true one. The amazing circus tumbling act on a remote farm road had been caused by ignorance of a law—a law that operates the same whether a truck, a boat, an airplane, or any moving body, is involved.

Sir Isaac Newton gave us the law, and it goes like this: "A body in motion tends to remain in motion until acted upon by an outside force." When the workers stepped off the back of the speeding truck, they were going the same speed as the truck itself. The outside force was gravity, which pulled them down to the road. But they were still traveling at the same speed as the truck, and—well, you get the idea.

They had been hurt, confused, frightened, and turned upside down because they didn't understand the principal law on which everything in the universe operates: the law of cause and effect.

This law has been written thousands of times by the greatest minds the world has produced, and, as a result, it has appeared in many forms. For our purposes, it might best be put this way: "Our rewards in life will always match our service." It's another way of saying, "As ye sow, so shall ye reap." And it's been written in many ways, in every language on earth.

Sir Isaac Newton, in promulgating his laws of physics, put it this way: "For every action, there is an equal and opposite reaction."

When you say, "Our reward in life will always match our service," you will almost always get general agreement. People will nod their heads and say, "Yes, that's certainly true." They will then go their ways and never realize, for the most part, that this truth is so great and all-enveloping that their every thought and action is affected by it.

I like to think of this law in the form of a giant apothecaries' scale—the kind with the cross arm from which hang two bowls on chains. One of the bowls is marked "Rewards"; the other is marked "Service," the world will "match" in the bowl marked "Rewards." How we think, work, talk, and conduct ourselves is what we have to put into the bowl marked "Service." And the extent and nature of our service will determine our rewards.

If any person alive is discontented with his rewards, he should examine his service. Action; reaction. "As ye sow, so shall ye reap." What you put out will determine what you must get back in return. It's so simple, so basic, so true—and yet, so misunderstood.

If a business is not expanding to the quick and exciting tempo of the times, it must examine its contribution—its service. If a person is unhappy with his income, he must examine and reevaluate his service.

Now, whom do we serve? Each of us serves a portion of humanity. And humanity, to any given person, is the people with whom he comes in contact. It is family, friends, neighbors, coworkers, customers, prospects, employers—all those he has chosen to serve. Everyone—everyone with whom we have any kind of contact—is to us humanity. And our rewards will be determined by the extent to which we serve.

Never before in the history of the world have human beings been so interdependent. It is as impossible to live without serving others as it would be to live if others were not constantly serving us. And this is good. The more closely knit this interdependence becomes, the greater will be human achievement. We need each other, and we literally cannot live without each other. Every time we strike a match, drink a glass of water, turn on the lights, pick up the telephone, drive our car, put on our clothes, take a bath, mow the lawn, or go fishing (try making your own fishhooks sometime), we're being served by other human beings. Every time we look at our watch, we are being served by a great industry, and by the efforts of thousands of human beings.

We all seek rewards, and we should understand that rewards come in two forms: tangible and intangible. That is, rewards include the money we earn, the home we buy, the car we drive, the clothes we wear; and they also include our happiness, our peace of mind, our inner satisfaction, the people we meet and enjoy.

But remember this: Whatever you seek in the form of rewards, you must first earn in the form of service to others. All attempts to sidestep this law will end in failure, frustration, and ultimately, demoralization.

We can see this frustration on every side. We can see it in the tense, strained, and nervous faces, and in the mountains of tranquilizers that are consumed every day. And we can see it also in the slack, bovine-like faces of those who have found the whole game too complicated and have simply given up—surrendered to the push and pull of circumstances.

How much of this do you suppose is due to the misunderstanding, or ignorance, of this simple and wonderful law of nature? It's my belief that a great deal can be traced to this cause.

Now, do *you* understand this law—fully understand it—intellectually and emotionally? If you do, you can chart a wonderful course through life.

Just as the field-workers stepped off the speeding truck, just as a child will put its fingers in the way of a closing door, just as a speeding driver discovers he's not going to make the curve; how many times have you been confounded because you acted contrary to the rules—not only the rules of man, but also the rules of nature? How many times have you been in the position of the man who sat in front of the empty fireplace and said, "Give me heat, and then I'll give you some wood"? People seem to be divided into those who understand that the wood must be put in before they can expect warmth and those who feel they should get warmth whether or not they do anything about it, or who feel they should get maximum heat from too small a supply of wood.

A person's discontent can be said to be measured by the distance between what he has and what he wants. Once that which is wanted has been achieved, the odds are good that still more will be wanted, for that's the way of people. And that's good; it's a healthy sign. Constructive discontent is what is responsible for our continuing upward spiral of civilization.

Let's assume you've determined what you want. Look objectively at the place in which you now find yourself, consider the distance separating you from your goal, and determine ways of increasing your service so you will build a bridge across it. This puts thought and creative activity into living. It also assures us that our goals can be achieved by individual effort—and in the shortest possible time.

One morning, I was having breakfast in a restaurant in Monterey, California—one of the most naturally beautiful places in the world. Suddenly, I was aware of the young couple sitting in the booth next to mine—they couldn't have been more than 25 years old. It was obvious that they were very unhappy. The young man was saying: "Well, I've tried everywhere, but nobody wants to give me a job. I guess we'll have to go back home."

It was apparent from their attitudes that they wanted to live on the Monterey Peninsula, but they were almost out of money and unable to find work. But he had said, "Nobody wants to give me a job." He wanted someone to give him something—in this case, a job.

What might have happened if he had turned the whole idea around? What if he had said instead, "What do I know how to do that will serve some of the people of this beautiful part of the world?" Or, "How can I, or we, be of value to this community?"

"The people here will be happy to supply us with the living we need if we can think of some way to serve them." *If we can* think *of some way to serve them.* "What do they need or want that we can supply? Do they need a handyman, a first-class housekeeper, or both? Can we wash and wax cars right in their driveways? Can we detail the cars so they look like showroom display models? Let's buy a pad of paper and a ballpoint pen and start making a list of all the things we can do to earn a living here. It will give us time to think of other ways, more profitable ways. But that wash-and-wax idea might grow into quite a service for the community. And let's not stop there. Let's think of some more ways we can start right here to be of service to the people who live here."

Right there in the restaurant, instead of being depressed and considering themselves failures, they could have come up with a dozen or so ways in which they could have remained on the Monterey Peninsula and built a fine business for themselves. They didn't need a job; they needed to *think.* But they had never thought before. It was as foreign to them as speaking Urdu.

There they were: two fine, bright, good-looking young people with two fine minds. A world of opportunity was beckoning to them, and they were going to go back home. No one had ever told them about the gold mines they carried between their ears.

Do you know how many people would have reacted in the same way these young people reacted? Most of the people in the United States—or any other country, for that matter. People will do everything in the world—even turn to crime—before they will think.

George Bernard Shaw once commented: "I have become rich and famous by thinking a couple of times a week. Most people never think at all."

The young couple in Monterey, conscientious as they were, were not sowing. Therefore, they could not reap. They were putting nothing into the community. Therefore, they could expect nothing in return. To some, this seems unfair, but it isn't. It's eminently and wonderfully and abundantly fair.

Our job is to do the sowing—that's our department. That's all. The rest will take care of itself. We've been given the equipment free and clear. All we are asked to do is use it. Unfortunately, thinking is not taught in the public schools—or in most of the private schools, for that matter. As incredible as it may seem, thinking is a subject that is totally ignored.

A person's world can be compared to a plot of ground. It exists; it's there. It has inherent within itself an astonishing potential, and it's prepared to react to a person's every action. In fact, it must.

Whatever your job happens to be, think of it for a moment as this plot of ground. In the beginning, there's nothing there but earth. If a person sits and watches it, nothing will happen to it. If a few seeds are tossed on it, the rain and the soil's natural fertility will combine to reward that person with a few results for limited efforts. Action; reaction. It all depends upon just what is wanted from this plot of earth. It's what is wanted that must first be decided.

Let's say what is wanted is a beautiful lawn, bordered by flower gardens, with a big tree, under the shade of which the person can sit one day and admire the work. So the areas for the gardens are marked off; the soil is cultivated, smoothed, and cleared of stones and trash; the lawn, flowers, and tree are planted. From this point on, anyone observing this plot of land can evaluate in a second the amount of service, the contribution, this person is giving to the project. How can you tell? You can tell by seeing what the land is giving back to the person.

We are given the plot, and that's all we should be given. Planting the plot is only the first step. How we tend it determines its degree of greatness and success.

There's a story about a preacher who was driving by a beautiful farm. The fields were beautifully cultivated and abundant with well-cared-for crops. The fences, house, and barn were clean, neat, and freshly painted. A row of fine trees led from the road to the house, where there were shaded lawns and flower beds. It was a beautiful sight to behold. When the farmer who was working in the field got to the end of a row near the road, the preacher stopped his car and hailed him. The preacher said, "God has blessed you with a beautiful farm."

The farmer stopped and thought a moment. Then he replied, "Yes, He has, and I'm grateful. But you should have seen this place when He had it all to Himself."

The farmer understood that he had been blessed with a fine farm; but he was also aware that it was his own love and labor that had brought it to its present state.

Each of us is given a plot to work—"a lifetime and the work we have chosen." Like the farmer, we can be grateful if we have the vision, imagination, and intelligence to build well and success-fully upon the seemingly unimpressive land of our beginnings. Or we can let it fall into a haphazard condition, with no real continuity or purpose behind it—with unpainted, ramshackle buildings, surrounded by weeds and debris. In both cases, the land is the same; it's what we do with it that makes the difference. The potential for a miracle is there, if only we're wise enough to see it and to realize that our fulfillment as persons depends upon our reaction to what we've been given.

To come up with ways to increase your service, read books on your specialty; read what others have found to work well for them. Make use of our resources. But at the same time, think of original and creative ways to increase your service—ways that are unique with you and the way you are.

Going at it strong for a week or a month and then falling back into old habits is just like working for a week or a month on that plot of ground and then abandoning it. Before long, it will be no better than before.

Each morning, and during the day, ask yourself this question: "How can I increase my service today, knowing that my rewards in life must be in exact proportion to my service?" Do this every day, and you will have started to form one of life's most valuable habits.

Horace Mann wrote: "If any man seeks for greatness, let him forget greatness and ask for truth, and he'll find both."

You can banish all the confusion and complications, nagging worries, and vague, half-formed fears by returning to the great truths, the great laws, the great verities on which all success, all accomplishment—on which the whole world—is built.

Drive down any street in the country—any street in any neighborhood or farm community—and you can quickly see what the people on that street are doing for the good of the community by observing what the community is doing for them. Have you ever looked at it that way?

When we look at a place of business, we can tell what it's doing for the community by observing what the community has done and is doing for the place of business. Is it thriving and growing? Or is it just holding its own? Or is it soon to go out of business? Whatever the situation, it's a reflection of its service—of how well its service, whatever it may be, is being accepted by the people. Is it meeting their needs and wants?

It's the same with families and their places of residence. That's why I said you could drive down any street. Some streets are lined with beautiful, expensive homes. Other neighborhoods are obviously suffering from poverty: Buildings are ramshackle; weeds are growing in the yards; tin cans and rubble are strewn everywhere; there are rusted cars. It's a reflection of what the people living in those homes—beautiful and expensive, or rundown and filthy—are doing for them and for the community. That's it.

It's always been a matter of interest to me that in neighborhoods with high unemployment, the people there don't seem to have enough time to keep their homes and yards tidy, while those who are working the hardest, doing the most, have the cleanest, most attractive homes, with well-manicured lawns and flower gardens. Environment is a mirror of the people in that neighborhood. Change the people, and the environment will change accordingly.

It reminds me of the old saying, "What you are speaks so loudly that I can't hear what you are saying."

One day, a man was watching a professional football game on television. His five-year-old son kept bothering him. So the man tore out a page of the Sunday paper. It was a full-page airline ad that showed a picture of the world—the planet Earth as seen from space. He tore up the page into a dozen pieces and gave them to his son. He said to him, "Here, put this picture together with this cellophane tape, and show Daddy how smart you are." He then went back to watching his football game.

In a surprisingly short time, the youngster had taped the picture back together. It wasn't very neat, but it was a very good job, indeed, for one so young. "Hey, that's amazing!" the father said. "How did you put that world together so quickly?"

The little boy said, "There was a picture of a man on the other side. I just put the man together, and then the world was all together."

The youngster was no doubt surprised by the big, warm hug he got. "That's right, son," the father said. "When the man is all together, his world is all together, too."

Being together is understanding how things work. Working hard won't do it. That isn't enough. We have to work intelligently. How often have we heard someone say, "My father worked hard all his life but never had anything to show for it"? It's another way of saying, "My father, may he rest in peace, never quite figured out how things work. He worked hard all his life, but it was at a job with very limited service." Or, in another case, it goes like this: "My father was a very bright person, but he kept jumping from one thing to another. He was always looking for the pot of gold at the end of the rainbow, but he never stayed with one thing long enough to work it out."

Succeeding takes time. It takes dedication, 100 percent commitment, and creative thought. We must keep asking ourselves, "How can I broaden my service and, by so doing, increase my harvest, my rewards?"

All right, how can we correct the situation? William James gave us the answer. He wrote: "Either some unusual stimulus fills them with emotional excitement, or some unusual idea of necessity induces them to make an extra effort of will.

"Excitements, ideas, and efforts, in a word, are what carry us over the dam."

All right. Let your goal represent the excitement. Your ideas and efforts will weigh down the service end of the scale. And the rewards must and will follow. They'll be yours—they are yours—the moment you realize this truth!

As you sow, so shall you reap, all the years of your life.

If you're worried about your income or your future, you're concentrating on the wrong end of the scale. Look at the other end; concern yourself only with increasing your service—with becoming great where you are—and your income and your future will take care of themselves. Don't be like the person sitting in front of that empty fireplace and asking for the heat; you're asking for the impossible. Pile in the wood first. The heat will come as a result.

Next time you're off by yourself in a quiet place, contemplate your plot of ground, your life, and begin to sow the seeds that will yield you a rich and abundant harvest.

In William James's essay "On Vital Reserves," he wrote: "Compared with what we ought to be, we are only half awake. Our fires are damped; our drafts are checked. We are making use of only a small part of our possible mental and physical resources." Stating the thing broadly, he went on to write: "The human individual thus lives usually far within his limits; he possesses powers of various sorts which he habitually fails to use. He energizes below his maximum, and he behaves below his optimum."

EXERCISES

1. Evaluate how effectively you are serving others now.

    _____

    _____

    _____

    _____

    _____

    _____

    _____

    _____

    _____

    _____

    _____

    _____

2. Note one major way in which you can increase your service
    today, knowing that your rewards in life must be in exact
    proportion to your service.

    _____

    _____

    _____

    _____

    _____

    _____

3. Assess whether you are working not only hard but also intelligently.

_____

_____

_____

_____

_____

_____

_____

_____

_____

_____

_____

_____

_____

6

SEED FOR ACHIEVEMENT

It is our intention that each of these messages be built upon a major principle, one of the great ideas that automatically produces the results we seek. In this message, let's talk about a principle that never fails. Adherence to this particular principle gives quality and richness to life. It also produces a peace of mind that never wavers. The principle is integrity.

Like other great principles, integrity gets a lot of lip service, but it's seldom a true way of life. How people love and value a person of integrity—integrity in everything he does—in all his relationships with others, in what he says, in his work.

When they hear the word *integrity*, people often conjure up a person of stern and sober visage who walks the straight and narrow. That's not the kind of integrity I'm talking about. I'm talking about integrity with a sense of humor, integrity with understanding, integrity with kindness and gentleness—but integrity all the same. Never expediency, never saying, "Well, everybody is doing it. I guess it won't hurt if I do it, too." But it does hurt. If it's wrong and we know it's wrong, it does hurt.

The "Seed for Achievement" is integrity. Integrity means honesty and the truth. Perhaps it was best put by Shakespeare. In a famous line in *Hamlet*, Polonius says: "And this above all, to thine own self be true. And it must follow as the night the day—thou canst not then be false to any man."

If we are true to ourselves, we cannot be false to anyone else. If our word to live by is *integrity*, we have what we need in a pinch, our sleep is untroubled, and we're respected wherever we go.

During the Korean War, the Chinese communists overran an American position and captured an American general. He was subjected to weeks of the worst kind of treatment, brainwashing and questioning. He never gave in. Finally, he was told that unless he answered their questions, he would be executed the following morning. That night, he wrote a letter to his wife. At the end of the letter, he said, "Tell Johnny the word is *integrity*." As it turned out, he was not executed, and he was later repatriated to American forces. But thinking he was going to die, he told his son that the word is *integrity*.

Integrity means to try, as best we can, to know ourselves, to examine ourselves as Socrates advised, and to make a true assessment of ourselves—an inventory of our abilities, our talents, our goals.

Not long ago, I received a letter from Scott D. Palmer, in which he said: "I came across some advice about happiness from my mentor, Dr. Brand Blanshard, that I published in my newsletter some time back. Blanshard is one of the greatest men of our century, even though few people have heard of him. He celebrated his 93rd birthday last year with the publication of his latest book, *Four Reasonable Men*, a biographical book on Marcus Aurelius, Joseph Ernest Renan, John Stuart Mill, and Henry Sidgwick. Appropriately, for Blanshard, the key virtue that leads to all the others is reasonableness."

Brand Blanshard is Sterling professor emeritus of philosophy at Yale University. On the subject of happiness, he wrote:

1. It is important to happiness not to think too much about it. The person who continually asks himself if he is happy is apt to miss his end. For happiness is, as Aristotle thought, a by-product of healthful and successful activity. Bertrand Russell, who wrote *The Conquest of Happiness*, remarked that scientists are generally happier that artists, since they are commonly lost in objective tasks and not examining their own navels. What is important is to find what one can do best (generally, also the line most useful to others) and then to do it with all one's might. Happiness will come unsought. If one seeks it directly, one will be like the discontented, rich old ladies who haunt Miami hotels.

2. The main principle of my ethics is: to act as to make the world as much better as possible. I have not lived up to it; no one has. [There I disagree with Dr. Blanshard;

he has made the world better, and so have many others.] But trying to live up to it involves constantly looking forward to the consequences of one's actions, choosing those that are likely to be fruitful, and inhibiting action from impulse. Many people think, of course, that acting on impulse is a requirement of happiness; and I agree that impulse must be there, the stronger the better, *provided it is under control*. But seeking happiness directly, by blindly following one's impulses, is too likely to end in hippiedom, drugs, and the gutter.

And the distinguished Yale professor wrote: "The *most* important thing I have learned is the necessity of reasonableness. The person who has the least to regret, who does most for his community, whose judgment carries the most weight and is the most trusted, is the person who is steadfastly and on principle reasonable. I don't mean the 'intellectual' who is often an impractical bore. I mean the person who, in matters of belief and matters of action, takes as his principle: Adjust your belief or decision to the evidence."

He completed his small essay on happiness by writing: "There is no one 'meaning of life.' No two lives have the same value. The richness of a life depends not on the amount of happiness it achieves, but on finding out who one is—i.e., about one's unique combination of powers—and then discovering through experiment and reflection what course of life will fulfill those powers most completely."

You will never get better advice. I agree with Scott Palmer that Brand Blanshard, Sterling professor emeritus of philosophy at Yale University, in his 93 years—most of them devoted to study and teaching and observing the human species—knows what he is talking about. And, to me, *reasonableness* is another word for *integrity*—integrity to truth, to the evidence, no matter where it leads. And I especially liked his comment, "The richness of a life depends not on the amount of happiness it achieves, but on finding out who one is—i.e., about one's unique combination of powers—and then discovering through experiment and reflection what course of life will fulfill those powers most completely."

What are your powers? There is something—probably several things—that you can do especially well, that you most enjoy doing, and that will, automatically, provide the greatest service to others. Are you ready to discover "through experiment and reflection what course of life will fulfill those powers most completely"? That's being true to yourself; that's integrity; that's reasonableness.

As a radio listener wrote to me one day, there is little we cannot accomplish as persons, if we manage the conquest of inner space.

Being truthful with ourselves means taking the responsibility of making the best use of what we have. And what do we have? We have our underutilized minds, our abilities, our talents, and time. These are our possessions. This is really an immense amount of wealth that belongs to each of us. And it's the investment of our wealth that will determine our rate of return.

Our mind, our abilities, our talents, and time. No one can take those away from us. We take them with us wherever we go, and they represent our true wealth. That's what makes the human being autonomous, although most people don't know it. They remind me of the horse or elephant that meekly does what it is told or directed to do. It is completely unaware of its own strength; it doesn't know how easily it could do what it wants to do. And millions of miraculous human creatures live in tiny prisons of their own fashioning, completely unaware of their powers to be free, to do what they would most love to do and, in so doing, to reap a harvest beyond their wildest imaginings. They are slaves to their ignorance and follow each other around and around like so many processionary caterpillars. How have they invested their wealth—their minds, their abilities, their talents, and their time? They're not even aware of it.

As with the ownership of wealth of any kind, it's left to us to decide what use we'll make of it. We can squander it until it's gone—spend it in a helter-skelter, hit-or-miss fashion without much purpose or meaning. Or we can invest it with intelligence and purpose and receive an abundant return—a return that will more than provide for our families all the years of our lives.

The choice is ours, and here is where integrity comes into the picture. We are the only ones from whom we can steal time, talent, ability, and the use of our minds. Integrity entails making the best use of what we have, what we *are*, in the time that has been granted us. Sound simple? The truth is always simple and uncomplicated.

As soon as we properly invest our true wealth, we place ourselves above competition. We're no longer competing; we're creating. We're understanding something that the great majority of people have never known. Here is the foundation upon which every great career has been built—in every field.

So invest in that yellow legal pad and a few ballpoint pens, and, in your own best quiet time, start jotting notes on how to make the best use of what you have.

Here are some givens in the success department: Success has nothing at all to do with the size of the brain. The largest brain on record was the brain of an idiot; the smallest, the brain of Anatole France, who won the Nobel Prize in literature in 1921. Some of the world's greatest people in every field are, or were, short, bald, and fat; some, tall and skinny. Some were brilliantly educated; some had little or no schooling.

The person destined for greatness is the person who decides for himself to play his strongest suit. But truly successful people all have one thing in common: They all follow, consciously or unconsciously, the law of cause and effect. They are true to themselves.

Although most people will give lip service to the principle of integrity, they're really not at all sure about it. With the great majority, it's often a matter of expediency. If it's expedient to be honest, fine; they're honest. If it's more expedient to realize a quick profit in some way by not disclosing the whole truth, or by shading it a bit, well, they shade it a bit.

They tend to live for short-term or even instant gratification. They don't see succeeding as a long-range program. They don't know about what I like to call the "unfailing boomerang."

Every time a person does something dishonest, whether it's small or large—whether it's stealing a pair of pliers from the plant or embezzling $10,000—he's throwing the boomerang. It's the same with small dishonesties, with manipulating the truth. How far the boomerang will travel, no one can tell; or how great or small a circle it will traverse, only time will tell. But it will eventually—inevitably—come around full circle and deliver its never-failing and painful blow.

Honesty, unfailing integrity, is good business. In fact, Mirabeau wrote that if honesty did not exist, we would have to invent it as the best means of getting rich.

It's absolutely true. And all we have to do under every circumstance is ask ourselves, "Is this true? Is this honest? Is this the best I can do?" And if it is, we can go ahead with the happy realization that we've put in motion the right cause, and know that the effect will take care of itself.

Our only hope of real success, of winning the hearts and minds of the people we serve, is in helping them in some way and, thus, improving their standard of living. But if we're content to give less than our best, we're actually working against ourselves.

The average working person in our society is paid for about 40 hours a week. This leaves 128 hours a week to do as he pleases. Never before in the history of humankind have we had so much free time. That's 128 hours a week—more than three times as much time as we spend on the job. How much is all that time worth? We need our sleep, and we want our leisure time, of course—time to relax, take it easy and recharge our batteries. But do we need 128 hours for that?

Our greatest enemy has never changed. Its name is ignorance. And the greatest ignorance of all is the mistaken belief that we can ever receive more than we truly earn. Sooner or later, there will be an accounting. Every day, for good or bad, we're throwing the boomerang. And just as the punishment always seems to be greater than the offense, the rewards are also out of all proportion to our honest efforts.

So let's summarize. What do we mean by integrity?

It means giving everything we do our very best.

It means being true to ourselves and to every person with whom we come in contact. This gives meaning and comfort to our leisure time—our rest has been earned.

We know we'll move ahead toward our goals simply because we become remarkable people. We cannot go unnoticed. The person of integrity is always needed, in every undertaking.

It means the willingness to keep an open mind, to look for truth wherever it leads all the years of our lives, to check things out for ourselves, to weigh what others tell us and to make our own judgments.

It's knowing that there is always a better way to do everything—and then a better way still to do that. It's looking for that better way in everything we do.

It's realizing that the person who does not read is no better off than the person who cannot read, and that a person who does not continue to learn and grow as a person is no better off than one who cannot.

We must walk with integrity every day of our lives, if we are to reap the abundant harvest all the years of our lives.

It's realizing that the greatest joy a human being can experience is the joy of accomplishment.

Remember to think of your life as a plot of rich soil waiting to be seeded. It can return to you only that which you sow. And what do you have to sow? You have great wealth: You have a mind; you can think. You have many abilities. You have talents that you still may not have explored. And you have time, which cannot be saved, stopped, or held back for a second. Make full use of these riches. It's never too late.

Use truth as your guide, have integrity as your banner, and your plot of ground will return to you and yours an abundance that will amaze and delight you.

And if you have days in which you find yourself depressed or confused, remember this comment by Dean Briggs: "Do your work. Not just your work and no more, but a little more for the lavishing's sake—that little more which is worth all the rest. And if you suffer, as you must, and if you doubt, as you must, do your work. Put your heart into it, and the sky will clear. Then, out of your very doubt and suffering, will be born the supreme joy of life."

EXERCISES

1. Reflect on your typical day. Can you spot an area where you are throwing an "unfailing boomerang"—where, for example, you are cutting corners you should not cut, or doing something you should not do? (Integrity, the "Seed for Achievement," is a deeply personal subject. Although space is provided for notes under this question, you may not want to write down a response. You may want to simply think it out, and make a mental commitment to take any corrective action that may be called for.)

_____

_____

_____

_____

_____

_____

_____

_____

_____

_____

_____

_____

_____

_____

_____

_____

2. Do you always look for the truth, wherever it leads? Do you check things out for yourself, weigh what others tell you, and make your own judgements?

_____

_____

_____

_____

_____

_____

_____

_____

_____

3. Write down a task that you consider difficult and/or unpleasant. Resolve to do it to the best of your ability, just for the joy of accomplishment.

_____

_____

_____

_____

_____

_____

_____

_____

_____

7

IT'S EASIER TO WIN

All kinds of studies have been made on the factors that motivate people to live as they do. In this book, we have already covered enough ground to establish the fact that people are responsible for their personal lives, barring some act of God or government—catastrophe or war—that might intervene to change things, permanently or temporarily. For example, a lot of my friends—many of them, very good friends—were killed during World War II, when they were in their 20s and 30s. The lives of others have been unalterably modified by injury or serious illness.

But most of us have our health, which is the natural inclination of all nature, and we have our lives to live. Sometimes, believe it or not, that's a personal handicap. It often takes the physically handicapped to demonstrate for us the options, the unlimited possibilities, that exist for those who are willing to set goals and stay with them until they're achieved. The healthy among us often take the path of least resistance.

I think it was Bill Veeck who, when he owned the Chicago White Sox, said, "I don't want the natural athlete. I want a guy who'll go after the hard ones." The people in this world who are willing to go after the hard ones are the people who achieve greatness. They are motivated (there's that word again) to give the last ounce of themselves in the achievement of their goals.

Now, let's look at some facts of life. Only about 5 percent of people achieve unusual success during their lives. These are the people who earn larger incomes, live in better neighborhoods—in better, larger homes—have better educations, enjoy more of the good things in life, and make correspondingly larger contributions to their communities. They tend to speak better English and send their kids to better schools.

There are always exceptions to any rule, and there are many exceptions to this 5 percent group. I know a man who is head of one of the largest, best-known companies in the United States, and who can hardly put 10 words together in their proper order. If murdering the English language were a crime, he would be on death row. Yet he has mansions, yachts, private jets—the works.

Why, with no more than perhaps a sixth-grade education, and the apparent determination to assiduously avoid any improvement on it, has this man enjoyed such spectacular financial success? Answer: he knows how to serve the people. His organization serves millions of people every day of the week. He has worked hard all his life to build the great organization he heads, and he has done a fine job of it. So he can buy $3 million yachts and pay cash for them. And when he wants to get someplace in a hurry, there's his Gulfstream III, warmed up and ready for him when his chauffeur takes him to the airport.

But most people in that top 5 percent fit the earlier description. Many of them are not rich by the standards of our megamillionaire friend, but their earnings fall into the top 5 percent of American incomes. They're set for life, and they, as a group, tend to enjoy themselves very much. They play a better game of golf or tennis than most of the country's duffers or hackers, and they love their lifestyles.

Now, when a child is born in the United States, according to the statistics we've been talking about, the odds are 95 to 5 that he will not be born in the top 5 percent. Like most children, he will soon take his environment for granted. Let's assume he's a boy—although it works the same way for a girl. (It will save my having to say "he or she" all the way through this interesting example.) He grows up accepting his environment, his world— and his world is his environment—as it is. Without his giving it a single thought, his environment becomes a natural part of him. Everything in his environment is a conditioning factor. The speech of his parents, relatives, and neighbors becomes his speech. What he learns in school will have very little effect on it. That's why you hear grown-up men and women who have gone through the American school system saying things such as "ain't" and "Where's it at?" They didn't learn those locutions in school; they were the habitual patterns of speech they had heard in their environment. (I know an attorney who still says, "Where's it at?")

Anyone's speech habits are an immediate tip-off as to his upbringing. The only reason mine tend to be rather good is because from the time I was a small child I wanted to be a writer, and words were of great interest to me. Words are the tools of a writer's trade, and a good writer will have a decent inventory of them and tend to keep them well-oiled and shining. I was the only person in our family so affected. The rest had other interests— education not being one of them.

If the statistics were reversed, it would be wonderful. If 95 percent of people were successful to the degree the 5 percent are, the odds of a child's being raised by the right group would be reversed. But that's not the case. So our typical young man grows up to mirror his environment. He thinks as the people in his environment think. He takes that life for granted. All the people he loves are in that group. It's his group, too. And if he doesn't come across some unusual motivation along the way, he will become an indistin-guishable part of it. he does that because it's the perfectly natural thing to do. Their goals (or lack of them) become his goals; a nice house on a nice street; a steady job of some kind; a good, steady income; a good wife and good kids. And so the story goes.

He operates on minimums all the years of his life. Except for times when he's engaged in sports or getting ready for a date, he never gets out of low gear. It isn't necessary to do so in the United States. This country is so affluent, so vital, and so peren-nially booming, that people don't have to shift into second or third gear to meet average requirements. And neither do most of the people throughout the world. Nor should they have to, if they don't want to.

His wife, while their children are small, is the hardest-working human being in our society. She doesn't have an eight-hour day or a five-days-a-week system. She works 16 hours a day, seven days a week. And according to a recent survey, if she had it to do all over, she would think twice about it. More than 50 percent of her number also hold down a regular paying job. She doesn't know about the 5 percent either.

No one ever said to this young man or to this young woman, "Now, look here: There two very distinct groups of people in our society. They are in different layers of this socioeconomic pyramid." And here, the parent, or a teacher, would have sketched a pyramid. "There is the top 5 percent, who live and work in this top section here," and the person would have drawn a line under what represents the top 5 percent of the pyramid. "Now, here is what we call the great middle class in America. It's divided into two main groups: the upper middle class"—another line would be drawn on the pyramid—"and the lower middle class. The United States has the largest middle class of any country in the world. And then, down here at the bottom—in these few lower layers—are the people who, because of a thousand perfectly good reasons, need to be helped by all the rest of us. They have difficulty coping. Many of them are too old or sick to help themselves. We have some 25 million functional illiterates," and so on.

So these young people would see, very clearly, their options. It would be made clear to them that, thank God and our forefathers, they have the freedom to choose. They have the option, if they so choose, to live and work on virtually any layer of that pyramid. And it should be pointed out to them that "The higher up on the pyramid you climb, the better the view, the fresher the air, and the smaller the crowd." That's important to know. "But it takes more effort to climb higher on a pyramid. It's much easier to settle for these lower layers. You don't have to learn so much," and so on.

"Now," the parent might continue, "we live right here, at this level on the pyramid." And then the parent might say, "It's not in the higher levels, but it's certainly not in the lower levels, either. It's where I wanted to be; your mother and I have been quite happy here. . . ."

Well, I hope you get the picture. Wouldn't it be wonderful if we would be shown that pyramid when we're about 12 or 13 years old? Wouldn't it be great to see that pyramid and know we have that option?

This book is for the people who want to be in the top 5 percent, and it contains a great deal of what we need to know to get into and stay in the top 5 percent. And while getting into the top 5 percent may be one's goal, it's good to remember that, like any destination on planet Earth, there are a million ways to get there. Any road will do, any calling will do, if we go about it in the right way. We can get rich hauling garbage, and many have already done so. It's a vital service to a community. But we have to go about it in a certain way.

This young man and, now that we've brought his wife into the picture, this fine young woman, because of their past environment—their conditioning—come under the statistics of "average Americans," for they live their lives in an average way. But, of course, they are not really average people. With the right motivation, they could become very uncommon people and do very uncommon things. They could render much greater service to their community, and reap a much more abundant harvest as a result, if they knew what we're talking about in this book.

What are the odds that they will ever come across Brand Blanshard's advice about happiness? Do they know what happiness is and where it comes from? Has either of them ever truly explored his or her potential strong point?

What does your original genetic pattern make you especially qualified to do, young man or young woman? What do you most want to do? What brings you the greatest joy? Do you know that your rewards, all the years of your life, will be determined by the extent of your contribution—your service to others? Do you know why some people are paid $20,000 a week, while others are paid the minimum wage? Bill Cosby earned $12 million in 1986. Do you know why? It's because of the people he serves. There's an investment banker in Los Angeles who earns about $40 million a year. Do you know that, as far as is known, there is no limit on earnings? What would you like to earn? How about $1,000 a week—that's $52,000 a year—or twice that? That's not all there is to living, by any means—far from it. But it does pay the bills. And if you earn an income that places you in the upper 5 percent of the population, there you are, in that top 5 percent of the pyramid that the sun hits first as the earth does its daily roll-over act. And the sun is still shining on it later in the day, when the rest of the plane is dark. It's nice up there. And shooting for it will bring out the best that's in you. You'll do more for others; you'll make a greater contribution; you'll give more to charities; you'll help more people. So how about it?

There's a talk I'd like to give to young people. Some would say I'd stir discontent among them, but I'd reply that discontent is the greatest motivator of all. And it's responsible for every great boon to humankind, from running water and the indoor toilet to the supermarket. A little discontent is a good thing—especially when it's discontent with ourselves.

The effect of environment is an incalculably powerful force. The deepest craving of young people in school is to be liked by their fellow students. Acceptance and esteem in the eyes of their contemporaries is their deepest craving. So they begin to do what the other kids are doing, and the other kids begin to do what they are doing, and everyone acts just like everyone else. They dress alike; they talk alike; they laugh at the same things—even when it isn't funny.

It's at this critical age that they begin to play a game called follow the follower (not follow the leader—that would be all right). Day after day, week after week, month after month, year after year, these young, wonderful, impressionable people conform to one another. They never ask, "Are the people to whom I'm conforming qualified to lead me?" What's important is belonging—belonging to the group.

And that's the subtle trap that gets practically everybody. If we don't break out of that trap, sooner or later, we will end in it. Millions—no, billions do. It's astonishing how many adults never break out. We see them in their 50s and 60s, still playing to the wrong crowd, still trying to be one of the gang.

Do you remember what Willy Loman said in Arthur Miller's great play *Death of a Salesman*? He said, "The important thing is to be liked." Willy Loman never grew up. He never knew who he was. His story is a modern tragedy. It's always been a tragedy. It's the story of the mob. . . .

When a person has no identity of his own, that person will seek to find his identity in a larger group. That's why joining groups of various kinds is so popular. In that way, we get a badge, a label, that tells us what we are. Now we are properly labeled. This is not to say that successful men and women do not belong to organizations. They certainly do, and they make major contributions to their organizations. But they don't need the organizations for identity. They are quite aware of who and what they are. And if their organizations did not exist, they would be successful, independent performers in society. They would never feel lost.

Successful people follow independent paths. This is the important point to remember. At some point in their lives, they break away from the crowd and start on a path of their own. That's the adult, the intelligent thing for human creatures to do. In striking off on an independent path, they are not necessarily alone. It's just that they join a much smaller group of like-minded people. We can't take the whole crowd into that top 5 percent.

The ancient Romans had their circus; modern Americans have their television. It's far superior to the old Roman circus, and they don't even have to leave the comfort of their living rooms. It's true that there are many wonderful things on television, and an eclectic approach—that is, selecting those programs in which you're really interested—makes sense. But millions of families have their television sets on all day. They are mesmerized by them.

And when one thinks of what they could be doing with some of that time, it makes one realize that "It's much easier to win."

One of the best things about getting into that top 5 percent is that as we get older, life need not become less interesting for us, or more laborious. We can become more productive as we approach our 60s and 70s and often many years beyond. And it's nice to grow older with all the goodies of life; it's more comfortable. One can spend one's winters in Florida, or somewhere south of the equator, and one's summers in the cooler, healthier climates. And one can enjoy all the benefits of the good life. But, perhaps most important of all, one can say, "I gave it my best, and I'm not through yet. It's been a wonderful experience, this holiday on earth. And I've enjoyed it very, very much. Now, let's see what I can do with the rest of it. Yes, I think it's actually easier to win. There's less competition up there, where the view is so much better, and the air is so fresh and clean."

And it's almost never too late, for with a purpose—a worthy goal—and the motivation to reach those upper layers on the pyramid, a person can travel farther in a few years than he might otherwise travel in a lifetime.

EXERCISES

1. Our environmental conditioning teaches us to conform, to
   play it safe. It's an easy trap to fall into—one that all of us fall
   into to some extent.

   In adulthood, do you ever find yourself playing the game
   Earl Nightingale calls "follow the follower"?

   _____

   _____

   _____

   _____

   _____

   _____

   _____

   _____

2. Analyze the key people in your environment, those who have
   an important effect on you in your family, in your community, at work, and socially. Who possesses qualities you want
   to emulate?

   _____

   _____

   _____

   _____

   _____

   _____

   _____

   _____

3. How can you improve your "human environment"?

_____

_____

_____

_____

_____

_____

_____

_____

_____

_____

_____

8

HOW MUCH ARE YOU WORTH?

Like most writers, when I see something I wrote 10 years ago, I invariably see ways it could have been improved. I didn't see those possibilities 10 years ago, but it's easier to see them today. It means that I've grown as a writer—that I'm better, that I'm a more effective writer today than I was 10 years ago. I'm worth more today. And if I continue as I have been doing, I will be much better and worth a lot more 10 years from now.

Before the atomic age, chemistry professors used to say that a person's worth, from a strictly chemical standpoint, was about $32 on the going market. In recent years, this view has undergone a startling change. Scientists now calculate that if the electronic energy in the hydrogen atoms of your body could be utilized, you could supply all the electrical needs of a large, highly industrialized country for nearly a week.

A Du Pont scientist said that the atoms of your body contain a potential energy of more than 11 million kilowatt-hours per pound. By this estimate, the average person is worth about $85 billion.

Moreover, the electrons in the atoms of your body are not just particles of matter; they are waves of living energy. And these waves ripple out and spread themselves in patterns of light, and as they move, they sing! If you had the proper hearing aid, you could hear a great flow, merging with the waves of neighboring atoms. Not only do they sing; they shine. If you would stand in front of an infrared television camera in a completely dark room, the screen would show you, from top to toe, as a glistening radiating, gleaming form.

In short, you're a whole lot more than meets the casual eye. Add to all this the fact that to try to reproduce your mind mechanically would cost many billions of dollars, and you begin to see yourself for what you really are: an amazing, infinitely valuable creature. And not only are you immensely valuable as a human being, but you also are unlike any other human who ever lived, or ever will live. You are unique.

Now, what are you selling all this for? All human beings are priceless, but the payments—tangible and intangible—they receive from life vary greatly. The purpose of this message is to help you decide just what you're worth as a human being right now, on the market, in today's society; and what you intend to be worth, say, oh, five years from now.

In the last analysis, every person is, in reality, in business for himself, in that he is building his own life, regardless of who happens to write his paycheck. So, for the purpose of this message, I want you to think of yourself as a business—as, let's say, a corporation.

You hold the office of president of this corporation, in that you are responsible for its success or failure. You and the members of your family are stockholders in your corporation, and it's your responsibility to see that the value of the stock increases in the years ahead. Your family has evidenced faith in you, and it's your responsibility to prove that their faith is justified. This is the job of any employed family member.

Now, while the operations of a corporation are multitudinous and complex, they can be reduced to four basic functions: (1) finance, (2) production, (3) sales, and (4) research. Without proper financing, there would be no production. Without production, the company would have nothing to sell. Without sales, it would have to completely stop production. Without research, it could not hope to keep abreast, or ahead, of our rapidly changing times. Slight any one of these four vital functions, and you have a deformed—a crippled—company. If you slight it long enough, you'll commit corporate suicide. . . .

We discuss finance—the money part of the whole thing—in another section. For now, let's concentrate on research, production, and sales. They are the head, hands, and legs of a company. We could say that the head handles research, the hands take care of production, and the legs handle sales. Cut off any one of these parts, and you're left with a shocked, staggering organization. How many once large companies and trade names can you think of that became giants and then disappeared entirely from the economic scene—names that once were world leaders in their fields and are now only memories? They failed to keep in balance these four crucial functions.

What about research for your personal corporation? Research can be said to exist for the improvement of two areas: present and future. That is, the research of a company should be devoted to ways and means of improving its present products or services, present production, and present sales. Future research is concerned with ways and means of developing new products or services, new methods of production, and new methods of marketing. But while this research is going on, present production must continue at a level as high as sales warrant.

In short, a corporation—your corporation—has two factors to consider: the present and the future. How successful you are in meeting these challenges will determine your present profits and your future growth.

Why are all companies concerned with growth—even when they seem to be doing well today? It's because of a law that operates with companies just as it does with human beings: Nothing in the world stands still—nothing in the entire universe stands still. A law of physics goes: "A body in motion tends to remain in motion, until acted upon by an outside force." A company that is growing has a tendency to continue to grow. (In other words, it's doing things right.) Conversely, a company that is going backward, or shrinking, has a tendency to continue to go backward, or shrink, until acted upon by an outside force.

All responsible company officers know that unless a company is growing, it's manifesting the first signs of death. You're the head of your personal corporation, and you should realize that this same law applies to you as well.

Now, just for a minute, let's take a look at the next 10 to 30 years. Before we do, keep this in mind: Just 10 years ago, if anyone had predicted that we would be living in the kind of world we have today, he would have been ridiculed. This includes everything—from our basic industrial technology to the luxuries and new products we take for granted, along with our present average income. We're reaching a point in the expansion of human knowledge where our advance is more than dynamic; it's explosive. Any prediction is very likely to be far on the ultraconservative side. But let's take a look at what the experts have to say.

According to many recent research studies, the next 10 years are going to offer business and the individual unlimited rewards.

In the next 10 years, the bulk of spending in the highly developed nations will be for products and services over and above the necessities—far above them. The necessities include clothing, shelter, transportation, and medical care. Imagine: Most of the spending will be for things above and beyond the necessities! This will be the first time this has happened in the entire history of the human race.

It's estimated the consumer market will expand 50 percent and more in the next generation or so—an astounding increase, soaring into the hundreds of billions of dollars.

In the next 30 years, for every building now in existence, a new building must be built.

And what about research and development, which is the future of our economy? Today, more money is being spent on R and D in a single year than was spent during the past 150 years.

Think for a moment: What does all of this mean to you and your own individual company—the one of which you are president? It means your future is unlimited, if you'll see yourself in relation to the present and the future. Never before, throughout all the centuries of man, has a person faced as bright a future as yours.

Our population is getting a lot smarter. Educational advances during the past 30 years have been remarkable. During the next 30, they'll probably be amazing! The customer is getting smarter every day. And if we're going to continue to meet his demands and sell him our products, we'd better get smarter every day, too.

The market of the next 10 years will be characterized by diversity—not uniformity. It will also be dominated by taste—not necessity. There will be a great increase in the quality as well as the quantity of consumer choices.

There are many signs of the increasing urge for the better things in life. Many millions of adults are currently interested in after-hours study programs, and this number is growing by millions each year.

Well, that's just a glance at a few of the things going on around us, and what life will be like in 10 to 30 years.

Now, each one of us—as president and unquestioned manager of our corporation—can decide what to do about it. We can either grow with it or go backward. We can't stand still—even if we'd like to! This gives us an opportunity to stand back and look at ourselves and our futures objectively—as an intelligent stranger might.

Ask yourself, "How much am I worth, right now, today, as a corporation? What is my value, today, to myself, my family and my company? If I were an outside investor, a stranger, would I invest in this corporation?"

A company growing at the rate of 10 percent a year will double in size in about eight years. What attention are you giving to the production of your personal corporation? Can you grow and improve as a person at least 10 percent a year? Of course you can. In fact, if we go along with the experts' estimates, a person can increase his effectiveness anywhere from 50 to 100 percent and more within 30 days!

Our files are filled with reports from people who exceeded their previous performance to an almost unbelievable extent: people in management and in production who multiplied their effectiveness many times; students who moved from failing grades to straight A's and the dean's list; people in sales who found they could, through the proper management of their abilities, minds, and time, sell as much of their company's products in a single month as they had previously sold in an entire year! Think what that means! It means being 12 times as effective as a human being. And, getting back to the law of cause and effect, it means putting out 12 times as much service, which must and will guarantee our receiving eventually 12 times the reward we formerly knew. Twelve times the reward!

Remember, please, that if we do twice as much, we have to receive twice as much. And nothing on earth can keep it from us. The same thing applies if we triple our effectiveness. You and I know this—everyone should know this. But remember that fully 95 percent of people do not know this. Think of the advantage this gives us. It isn't that we want to take advantage of anyone— and we're not. But it dramatically demonstrates the truth of the saying: "Knowledge is power."

You would be amazed by the great numbers of people who stop learning when school is over. Aside from company manuals and other internal literature, they read very little or anything of real value. The introduction of recorded learning, pioneered by this company, has made substantial gains and is growing rapidly, but as yet, it has only scratched the surface. An ongoing education is vital, if we are to stay vital. There's so much to learn, and our school curriculum touched only a fraction of it. One of the most important subjects is getting along with people. We can do things, we can win, only through people, and that subject isn't taught at all in school. The great ideas we're talking about in this book are seldom taught in the home, and almost never in school.

Go through our list of resources carefully. With them, one by one, you can maintain an effective, ongoing education program for many years to come.

It's true: Knowledge is power. What's more, knowledge shows on our faces, and it's apparent in our speech. It helps us raise our children, and get along better with our neighbors and fellow workers. Above all, perhaps, it's the greatest motivator in the world. As we learn, our horizons recede; we realize there is more to do, and more time in which to do it. Old myths about getting out of action at age 65 are dispelled, and we realize that as long as we're learning and growing, it need never stop, and we become more effective with the passage of time.

Tomorrow is a brand-new day. Time is the great equalizer—you have no more, or no less, than anyone else on earth can have. Right now, begin to think of ways in which you can begin to increase your effectiveness, raise your production, knowing that by so doing, you're automatically presetting your rewards. Each day that comes to you, beginning with tomorrow, offers you a clean, brand-new page on which to write the story of your life.

Forget the past; it's gone. Don't concern yourself with the opportunities you may have missed in the past . . . but reach out and take each new day as it comes, and ask yourself, "How can I best use this day?" As you know, we're going to run out of days eventually.

If we waste an hour of productive time every day, it adds up to about 250 hours a year that our corporation, our plant, is shut down. We can earn nothing with the doors closed. What is your time worth an hour? Multiply this by 250, and you can see what you're throwing away. Now, whether or not your employer pays for this wasted hour is unimportant. Life will not pay for it.

Learn to enjoy every minute of your life. Be happy now. Don't wait for something outside of yourself to make you happy in the future. As my good friend Wally Amos, of Famous Amos Chocolate Chip Cookies says, "Happiness is an inside job." Think how really precious is the time you have to spend, whether it's at work or with your family. Every minute should be enjoyed, savored.

A human life is really nothing more than a collection of minutes, hours, and days. These are the building materials. And it's left strictly up to us to determine the kind and size of structure we build.

A person has a tremendous advantage over even the largest corporation. Think of any large multinational corporation. Can it double its production in a single day? Of course not. Can it double its sales in a single day? Of course not. It would like to, but its growth must be gradual and steady, because of the interconnecting complexities of operating so large an organization. Yet a person can double, triple, or quadruple his effectiveness in a month or less. It's like comparing the movement of a single scout to the movement of a great army.

How have you been handling the four vital functions of your business: finance, research, production, sales? How much time and effort are you giving to finance? To research—to the study of your work, your career? Can this be improved? What about production? How can you vastly improve the way in which you conduct your work? And how can your sales be improved? Sales entails more than selling a product or service; it includes the way in which we sell ourselves to everyone with whom we come in contact. It includes the way we get along with our associates, our spouse, our kids, our neighbors.

And if our business happens to be selling, how can we see more people every day, or improve the effectiveness of every part of our contact? One extra call a day comes to 250 calls a year. How many additional sales could we make with 250 additional contacts? In five years, that comes to 1,250 calls we would not otherwise have made. It's the difference between being average or above average. It's the difference between being good and great.

Taking this new, active approach to life brings peace to our minds, absolute security to our futures, and great new stature as human beings. In this way, we can work toward reaching full maturity.

With this attitude toward life, we need never for a moment concern ourselves with its outcome. We'll begin to become successful tomorrow, and we'll enjoy an abundance for the rest of our years.

EXERCISES

Analyze your worth as a one-person corporation in three of four critical areas of operation: research, production, and sales. Then write down ways in which you can improve in each of these areas.

1. How are you doing in research? (For example, are you holding a regular career study hour?)

    _____

    _____

    _____

    _____

    _____

    _____

    _____

    _____

    _____

    Plans for improvement:

    _____

    _____

    _____

    _____

    _____

    _____

    _____

    _____

2. How is your production? (Are you spending an hour a day brainstorming? Are you putting the best of these ideas to work to increase your productivity? Are you more productive, more effective, on the job this year than you were last year? Art you growing and improving every year?)

Plans for improvement:

3. How are you doing in sales (that is, selling yourself and your ideas to others, relating to others)?

_____

_____

_____

_____

_____

_____

_____

_____

Plans for improvement:

_____

_____

_____

_____

_____

_____

_____

_____

_____

9

LET'S TALK ABOUT MONEY

Let's talk about money. Men and women have been concerned about money since the first coin was fashioned in Asia Minor about 700 B.C. You might say that money is like good health, in that we are concerned about it to the extent that we don't have it.

The purpose of this message is to get down to the basics—to clear the air surrounding the entire subject of money. To do this, I'm going to have to get absolutely elementary. And while you may already know most of the things I'm going to say, I think it's important that we remind ourselves just exactly what money is, how much of it is enough, and how to earn the amount of money we need to live the way we want to live, now as well as in the important future years.

To begin, let's dispel the old myth, once and for all, that money is bad or unimportant. It is not bad, and it is important—it is vitally important. It is just as important as the food and clothes it buys, the shelter it affords, the education it provides, and the doctor's bills it pays. Money is important to any person living in a civilized society. To argue and split hairs to the effect that it is not as important as other things is absurd. Nothing will take the place of money in the area in which money works. That's all there is to it.

What is money? Money is the harvest of our production. Money is what we receive for our production and service as persons, which we can then use to obtain the production and services of others. We can quite often accurately gauge the extent of our production and service by simply counting the amount of money we receive for it.

You will hear people say, "Money won't bring happiness." The earning and possession of money has brought a lot more happiness than poverty has. Money is a warm home and healthy children; it's birthday presents and a college education; it's a trip abroad and the means to help older people and the less fortunate.

We are not saying that just piling up a lot of wealth is important. What we are saying is that money is important because it's the only reward that is completely negotiable and can be used by everyone.

Look at it this way: A diamond is more valuable than a lump of coal is; yet that's exactly what a diamond was at one time. And just as a lump of coal can be transformed into one of the world's most valuable gems, a human being can vastly increase his own value to the world.

Try to remember this formula: The amount of money we receive will always be in direct ratio to the demand for what we do, to our ability to do it, and to the difficulty of replacing us.

In our economy, a highly skilled human being is worth more money than is a person who is not highly skilled and who can be easily replaced. This is not to say that one person is any better or more important than any other person. Remember that, in this message, we're talking about only money—nothing else.

A janitor is just as important, as a human being, as a brain surgeon is. But the amount of money they will earn will be proportional to the demand for what they do, their ability to do what they do, and the difficulty of replacing them. In a few weeks, a person can be trained to clean and maintain a building, and replacing the person is not difficult. A brain surgeon spends many years learning his profession—often at great personal sacrifice and at extremely high cost—and he cannot be easily replaced. As a result, the surgeon might earn as much money in an hour as a janitor might earn in a year.

Now, these are extreme cases used to show the relation of income to demand, skill, and supply. But this is as it should be.

There are few limitations on a person within his company and industry. But his income will be in exact proportion to the demand for what he does, his ability to do what he does, and the difficulty of replacing him. That's why the whole idea of trying to get something for nothing is ridiculous—and won't work.

In a year, a top jockey will earn a great deal of money, which will represent about 10 percent of the winnings of the horses he rides. You might say that riding a racehorse serves no useful purpose, but, useful or not, the demand for it is there. It's the same with a star in show business—his income will very accurately reflect the demand for what he does.

That's why preparation for life is so important. As we mentioned, luck has been defined as what happens when preparedness meets opportunity. A great opportunity will only make the unprepared, the unqualified, appear ridiculous. For every one of us, opportunities are all around us. Our ability to see them will depend, in large part, on how well we have prepared ourselves.

Now, how do you stack up in this regard? While this may sound elementary, you'd be amazed at the number of people who want more money but don't want to take the time and trouble to qualify for it. And until they qualify for it, there's no way on earth for them to earn it! It's like the person who wants a good-looking figure but doesn't want to change his eating habits.

To nine-tenths of the world's population, the average North American is already rich. There's a greater difference between the standard of living of most of the world's population and our average worker than there is between the standard enjoyed by our average worker and the richest person in our society.

Most of our working people have just about everything our wealthiest have—only on a smaller scale. They have a home, a car—often two of them—a radio, a TV, a savings account, and debts; they're just smaller. Their food is just as good and is just as plentiful in their homes. Their beds are just as comfortable. Their home is just as warm in the winter. They have exactly the same amount of time and just as much—maybe more—freedom. Their life expectancy at birth is about 75 years. For the rest of the world, on the average, it's less than 60.

With only a fraction of the world's population, we in the free world have half of the world's total money income. We have more than two-thirds of all the automobiles on the planet. So, in talking about money, let's understand that we're already rich, as people.

Now, how much do *you* want? How much money do you need to live in the way you want to live, to accomplish the goals you have established for yourself?

Most people think they want more money than they really do, and they settle for a lot less than they could earn if only they went about it in the right way. The world will pay you exactly what you bargain for—exactly what you earn—and not a penny more.

Do you remember the old poem that goes: "I bargained with life for a penny, and life would pay no more"? Well, that's about it. We will receive not what we idly wish for but what we justly earn. Our rewards will always be in exact proportion to our service. If you don't like your income, you must devise ways and means of increasing your service. Your service must come out of you— your mind, your abilities, and your energy.

A strong person cannot make a weak person strong; but a weak person can become strong on his own by following a specific course of action for a sufficient length of time. And a person who's already strong can become a lot stronger. . . .

People who refuse to do more than they're being paid for will seldom be paid for more than they're doing. You may have heard someone say, "Why should I knock myself out for the money I'm getting?" It's this attitude that, more than anything else, keeps people at the bottom of the economic pile. They don't understand that only as we grow in value as persons will we receive the increased income we seek. If we try to stand still in our work—and millions do—we'll never know the rewards, or the joy, of accomplishment, and the personal satisfaction and peace of mind that come only to the person of unusual achievement.

There are two distinct steps we must take. First, we must decide exactly how much money we really want. Once this decision is made, the second step is to forget the money and to concentrate on improving what we now do, until we've grown to the size that will fit and naturally earn the income we seek.

Once we're fully qualified for the amount of money we've decided to earn, we'll soon find ourselves earning it. And we'll also discover that with our new powers and abilities, it's not more difficult—it's perhaps even less difficult—than what we're now doing for the money we're now earning.

Ask yourself, "How much money am I perfectly willing to earn (realizing that the amount I earn will be in exact proportion to my skills, the demand for what I do, and the difficulty of replacing me)?"

There are really three amounts of money a person should decide upon: (1) the yearly income he wants to earn now—or in the near future; (2) the amount of money he wants to have in a savings and/or investment account; and (3) the amount of money he wants as retirement income—whether or not he ever retires from active work.

Now, it's here that most people make a very serious mistake: They never decide on any of these three amounts of money.

If you will decide on these three amounts, and if you will write them on a card to carry with you, or to put somewhere where you can review it from time to time, you will automatically have placed yourself in the top 5 percent of people. You will have a plan for your future—a blueprint for future financial accomplishment. You will know where you are going, and if you are serious about it, you will most certainly get there.

You see, the trouble with people is not that they can't achieve their goals—they can do that, all right. The trouble is that they don't set goals. They leave their future to chance and find out, sooner or later and to their sorrow, that chance doesn't work—that they've missed the boat.

It's estimated that only 5 percent decide on the money they'll earn—and then grow as persons to earn the incomes they seek. Thus, they take their lives, their fortunes, and their futures into their own hands—as they should—and accomplish their goals, right on schedule, all the years of their lives. You can do the same thing, and you can do it starting right now!

Where money is concerned, there are two kinds of people: those in the majority who cut back on their wants to fit their incomes; and those free spirits in the minority who make their incomes fit their wants. Now, which is better for you? You must decide.

Ben Franklin gave us the secret to wealth. He said that the road to wealth lies in augmenting our means or diminishing our wants. Either will do. But the quickest way to wealth is to do both at the same time.

When you write down the yearly income you want to earn, you no doubt know whether or not it's average or above average for the work you're in. The chances are good that the figure you'll decide upon will be above average—perhaps quite a bit above average. That's good! Now ask yourself, "Who in my line of work is now earning that kind of money?" If you know, you'll have a good idea of what you have to do to earn it.

This is exactly how men and women move from the ranks into positions of top authority, with corresponding incomes.

I have no way of knowing your line of business. Regardless of the business you're in, it needs new leaders—men and women to come up in the years ahead. Everything is expanding, getting larger, and with the increase in size and scope, the most desperate need is for the dedicated, able person who can learn to lead—to *lead the field*—and to lead others as well.

Some of the top executives in the nation today were once accountants, shipping clerks, struggling lawyers, service-station attendants, salespeople in the field, salesclerks, mailroom clerks, stenographers, mechanics. You cannot think of a position from which people have not climbed to the top.

Understand what I'm going to say, and it will bring you and yours everything you want: It's not the job; it's the person. It's not your present circumstances that count; it's the circumstances you make up your mind to achieve that are important. The only limit on your income is you. And the income you decide upon can be achieved within the framework of your present work, or within the industry or profession where you already have a start and a place. If not there, it can be found somewhere else.

All you need is a plan—the road map—and the courage to press on to your destination, knowing in advance that there will be problems and setbacks, but knowing also that nothing on earth can stand in the way of a plan, backed by persistence and determination.

With the income that you intend to earn written down on a card, spend a part of each day thinking of ways in which you can increase your service, knowing that you have only to manage this, and the income will take care of itself. Since the amount of money you want to earn is more than you're now receiving, your part of the bargain is to find ways of increasing your service until the gap has been bridged—and more than bridged!

Look at your card with the three amounts written on it. By setting a financial goal, you are demonstrating faith in your future. You'll find that you'll begin to become what others call "lucky." You'll begin to get good hunches and ideas. You'll take far more interest in everything about your work and your company. You'll see opportunities in your work and environment that you've never noticed before. In fact, you'll soon discover that you're no longer the same person. You'll care less about how others are doing their jobs and concern yourself more with the manner in which you do yours. By your example, you'll inspire others to do their jobs better.

Have faith in yourself—and the quiet, firm, inner knowledge that you can and will accomplish your goals. Know that the answers you seek will come to you in their own time, if only you keep looking for them.

Above all, realize that money cannot be sought directly. Money, like happiness, is an effect. It's a result of a cause, and the cause is valuable service.

Keep money in its proper place. It's a servant—nothing more. It's a tool with which we can live better, see more of the world, give our youngsters the education they need and a good start in life. It's the means to a happy, carefree retirement in later years. Money is necessary to modern life, but keep it in its place. You need only so much food to enjoy good health; you really need only so much money to live comfortably, securely, and well. Too much emphasis on money reverses the whole picture; you then become the servant, and the money becomes the master.

As someone once put it: "It's good to have money and the things money can buy, but it's good, too, to check up once in a while to make sure that you haven't lost the things that money can't buy."

Every person should know happiness in his work and home, and prosperity. These things can and should be yours. Reread this chapter as often as you can during the next week. Fix your plans firmly in your mind and relax. Keep cool and calm. Be as serene as you possibly can be. You have nothing to worry about.

Right now, you may have no idea at all how the additional income you seek is going to come to you, or how you're going to save the amount you want in a savings account, or how you can possibly arrange for the retirement income you've decided upon. That isn't important. Remember that the only really important thing is that you know what you want. If you do, you will become—you *must* become—what you think about.

Be realistic about your financial goals, for as you reach them, you can then set higher goals. Trying to jump too far too soon can often result in confusion, tension, and worry. Take your growth in sensible, logical steps, remembering that the big thing is that you know what you want, that you realize your rewards will match your service, and that you can devise ways and means of becoming the person who is worth the amount of money you have established for yourself.

A person may be worth more than he's getting—for a while—but the two will match up. They have to. In fact, unless a person is worth more than he's receiving, he cannot move ahead.

He's receiving all he's worth.

It all gets back to the great law that controls everything in the universe: cause and effect. The cause must precede the effect, or the effect cannot occur. This is why people who try to get something for nothing are only fooling themselves and earning the disillusionment and frustration they must one day reap.

You can have what you want. You need only make up your mind.

EXERCISES

1. How much money do you want? How much do you need to
    live in the way you want to live?

    There are three amounts of money that you should decide
    upon: (1) the yearly income you want to earn now or in the
    near future, (2) the amount of money you want to have in a
    savings and/or investment account, and (3) the amount you
    want as retirement income.

    Set your financial goals.

    Yearly income:

    _____

    Financial reserves:

    _____

    Retirement income:

    _____

2. Who in your line of work is now earning that amount of
    money? (If you know, you'll have a good idea of what you'll
    have to do to earn it.)

    _____

    _____

    _____

    _____

    _____

3. Continue to make plans for increasing your service to others, for making yourself more valuable. The money will follow!

_____

_____

_____

_____

_____

_____

_____

_____

_____

_____

_____

_____

_____

10

ONE THING YOU CAN'T HIDE

I'm sure you'll agree that we acquire the skills of living successfully through knowledge. Knowledge, properly applied, is power—and knowledge is available to everybody.

The degree of a person's ignorance will determine his place in the world. Everyone is born ignorant and must, for a time, live in ignorance. But remember this: Anyone who remains ignorant has only himself to blame.

In our society, an illiterate person is in the lowest level of our social heap. From that starting point, think once again of society as that pyramid, with a broad base, gradually rising to a high point. We know that the great majority of people are to be found in the bottom, large layers of this pyramid. The higher you go, the smaller the layers. At the very peak of the pyramid, you'll find the world's most brilliant people. We may not have the native equipment to reach the pinnacle—although we certainly might—but we do control where we will live between the very top and the very bottom. We can, most assuredly, get into the top 5 percent. And from there, we can live well and successfully all the days of our lives. It isn't that we want to be over anyone; it's just that we have the ambition and good sense not to settle for anything less, to want to live the best we can.

Remember, the higher you climb on a pyramid, the farther you can see, the fresher the air, and the less crowded it becomes. Another rewarding thing about climbing is that as we climb, we help most of those associated with us to climb, too.

One of the most important ladders leading to the top is knowledge. The more we know, the higher we can climb. But where does a person begin? No one person can know everything—in fact, our store of knowledge is growing far too fast for anyone to keep up with it. It's like walking into the Library of Congress, with its millions of volumes, and trying to decide which single book to read first—knowing that even if we lived a thousand years, we couldn't read them all.

Fortunately, the answer to this perplexing problem is known: A person should begin with the study of his language, and then study his general area of interest. Those two steps, in that order, can move us right up there, to the top of the pyramid.

First, the language—in our case, English. Not enough people realize that it is our ability to use our language that will determine our place on the social pyramid—and that will also control, to a great extent, the amount of money we will earn during our lives.

A person may dress in the latest fashion and present a very attractive appearance. So far, so good. But the minute he opens his mouth and begins to speak, he proclaims to the world his level on our pyramid. George Bernard Shaw's play *Pygmalion*, which was later adapted into the musical comedy *My Fair Lady*, is an extreme example of what I'm talking about.

Our use of our language is the *one thing we can't hide*.

Many years ago, the graduating class of a large university was given an examination in English vocabulary. The test scores were graded into groups of 5 percent—the top 5 percent, and so on to the bottom. At regular intervals during the next 20 years, questionnaires were sent to the surviving graduates, asking them their occupations, incomes, and so on. Without a single exception, those who had scored the highest on the vocabulary test were in the top income group, while those who had scored lowest were in the bottom income group.

Reader's Digest published an article by Blake Clark titled "Words Can Work Wonders for You." In it, he wrote: "Tests of more than 350,000 persons from all walks of life show that, more often than any other measurable characteristic, knowledge of the exact meanings of a large number of words accompanies outstanding success."

In his article, Clark also mentioned the work done in this field by scientist Johnson O'Connor, and he gave O'Connor's best illustration of the importance of vocabulary: Tests were given to executive and supervisory personnel in 39 large manufacturing plants. The results showed that every one of the people tested rated high in the basic aptitudes that go with leadership. Differences in their vocabulary ratings, however, were definite and dramatic. Presidents and vice presidents averaged 236 out of a possible 272 points; managers averaged 168; superintendents, 140; foremen, 114; floor bosses, 86. In virtually every case, vocabulary correlated with executive level and income.

Children with the best vocabularies get the best grades in school.

A salesman in his 50s who scored in the bottom 5 percent in vocabulary worked himself into the top 45 percent, and he is now vice president of his firm.

"An encouraging fact to keep in mind," Blake Clark went on to say, "is that when we master one word, we find that we have added several others. It's as if the new one is a nucleus of thought around which whirl numerous related ideas that we now come to understand. Deliberately learning 10 new words, we pick up probably 90 more, almost without realizing it."

You see, understanding our language is the key to studying and learning everything else.

Literally millions of people are being held back in life simply because they've never taken the time to learn their own language.

Let's face it: From the earliest times, the favored class of people has always been the educated class. They can make themselves recognized instantly, anywhere, by the simple expedient of speaking a few words. Our language, more than anything else, determines the extent of our knowledge.

You see, everything in all the vast storehouse of knowledge has a name, a label. These names, these words, make up the language. The more words we know and can properly use, the more knowledge we have. Of this you can be sure: A person's knowledge and his vocabulary go together. It's almost impossible for one to be greater than the other. . . .

Make it a point to acquire books that will help you improve your vocabulary. You'll find them valuable additions to your library and an enormous help in your career.

In addition to vocabulary, effective English usage is important. This entails learning the parts of speech, what they mean, and how they should be used to construct sentences. Your usage, too, is a reflection of your present knowledge.

Right now, mentally rate yourself on your knowledge of your language. Would you say your rating is "excellent," "good," "fair," or "poor"?

If you rated yourself "excellent," you're in the top 0.1 percent of the population. If you said "good," you're already definitely in the top 5 percent. If you rated yourself "fair," get a good book on

English at your bookstore, and study it. And if you rated yourself "poor," take a home-study or night course in English. Many excellent courses are available.

Impress on your youngsters the importance of knowing their language, the importance of speech.

More people speak English now than any other language on the planet, with the possible exception of Chinese. English (and American) literature, from Chaucer to Eliot, from Shakespeare to Hemingway, is the richest and most extensive on earth. So when you're studying English, you're studying one of the world's greatest languages and most interesting subjects.

If you think you don't have time to study, listen to what Louis Shores has to say: "Each of us must find his own 15-minute period each day for reading. It's better if it's regular. The only requirement is the will to read. With it, you can find 15 minutes, no matter how busy the day. That means you will read half a book a week, two books a month, 20 a year, and 1,000 in a reading lifetime. It's an easy way to become well-read." And it takes just 15 minutes a day.

Now let's discuss our second area of study: our general interest. Everyone has a main interest. This is true of the salesperson, doctor, architect, executive, or student. Reading in this area is for profit. We should read for pleasure as well.

Once we have a regular program to improve our knowledge of our language, we should begin a systematic study of the field that interests us most and that will help us reach our goal just that much sooner.

I received a letter from a woman who listens to my radio program. In her letter, she said it was her ambition to write poetry. There was a telephone number on the letterhead, so I called her. I asked her how long she had been studying poetry, and what kind of a collection of published poetry she had. She told me she didn't have a single book on poetry and had never read it as a study.

I mention this because it's so often the case. People will say they want to do a particular thing, but a bit of questioning quickly reveals that it's a whim—not a real and important goal to them.

If we're interested in boating, we subscribe to boating magazines, and usually have a collection of books on boating, stories of the sea, a collection of the works of Joseph Conrad, and we usually know, down to the bilge pumps and mooring lines, exactly the kind of boat we want. I know, because I have such a collection. I also have a wonderful collection of books on English, including several excellent dictionaries, a number of books on writing and style and mistakes to avoid, as well as poetry, great fiction, the Great Books of the Western World.

Most languages can number their words under 200,000. The English language has more than 600,000 and is still growing every day. None of us can learn them all, although professors of English come very close. Incidentally, the person who ranks second in the country in the use of his language is the corporation president, and that's no accident. Our ability to translate our thoughts and ideas into words, in a powerful and effective way, is inextricably linked to our growth in the world of business, or any other organization.

In addition to English, each of us should have a good working knowledge of world history and, especially, the history of our own country and the history of the idea of human freedom. Millions of Americans don't know how truly fortunate they are to be able to openly criticize their government and its leaders, to be able to bring suit against public officials, to call an attorney of their choice in case of arrest, and to be judged by a jury of their peers.

Do you know that as far as is known, there has never been a verdict of innocent in a Soviet court? If you go to trial in the Soviet Union, believe me, you're found guilty, and you're going to prison or a work camp. In hundreds of countries, you could be subjected to torture without recourse.

Some years ago, my wife and I were talking to a couple in South Africa, a white couple, and they said to us, with feeling, "My God, when the plane lands in the United States, you can smell the freedom."

Most Americans, believe it or not, don't know anything about the idea of personal liberty, or how difficult it was to come by, or how precious it is. Nor do they have the foggiest notion of their true options and opportunities.

I think a good personal library is essential. It should contain good books and a dozen or so excellent audio programs. The audio program is the greatest innovation in learning since the invention of the printing press. It's effortless, yet so effective. When you listen to the human voice, you're learning in the way you learned most of what you know. It's the most natural way to learn. And while a book is often read only once, audio programs can be easily listened to over and over, months and years later. You can listen to them while you're doing other things—dressing in the morning, driving the car, having a snack, or sitting at the dinner table, so that the entire family can soak up some information.

Those without a good library—and they don't even build bookshelves in American homes anymore, unless they're specified by an architect—are seriously handicapped. They miss so much of the fun, the joy, of learning the things we want to learn. Books and audio programs are not an expense item. They're an investment—and, as far as we know, the best investment on earth. They pay us dividends out of all proportion to their small cost—and not only in pleasure and knowledge, but also in cash, in income.

As someone has written: "Books extend our narrow present back into the limitless past. They show us the mistakes of the men and women before us and share with us recipes for human success. There's nothing to be done which books [and let me add audio programs] will not help us do much better."

To try to live without constantly expanding our knowledge is to close our eyes—not just to the whole purpose of life, but to the facts of life as well. Never before has the world moved so rapidly as it's moving today. We must make up our mind to move with it, to stay up with it, to grow and prosper with it, or to just fall by the wayside. It's not only because expanding our knowledge is the best way to our goals, but also because it's the way to really enjoy living—as the skillful sailor enjoys the sea.

So often, a person will live in the shallows from force of habit—or because those around him are wasting their time—without realizing that only a thin screen of reeds separates him from the fine, deep ocean beyond. He can sail to any chosen port—if he has taken the time and expended the effort to build a good boat.

Now let me make an important point. The person who knows where he is going, and who has made up his mind to get there, is going to make the grade, regardless of education. If an education is necessary to the accomplishment of his goal, he will get it. Nothing in the world can take the place of persistence and determination.

Yet I think it's important to succeed in every department of our lives, and becoming well-educated is one of the most vital. What good is a large material success if a person has remained too ignorant to enjoy it? Or to administer it?

Now let's recap:

Knowledge is power. The greater your knowledge, the more power you can exercise over your life and your future.

Think of human society as a pyramid, composed of layers— beginning with a broad base and narrowing to a pinnacle. Pick the place on the pyramid you're going to shoot for, and start climbing.

Since there's far too much knowledge for any one person to as- similate, where can you start? First, with your language, and next, with your general area of interest—two subjects that can keep you growing and interested for the rest of your life.

Remember that your language is the one thing you cannot hide— except by silence. Bring it up to the point where it can do the job you want it to do for you.

To a surprising extent, your ability to use your language and the extent of your vocabulary will determine your income and your future.

Spend at least 15 minutes every day reading something not only interesting, but also calculated to stretch your mind a little more. Remember that a mind stretched by a new idea can never again return to its original dimensions.

It's estimated that the average person adds only five words a year to his vocabulary. That's not nearly enough for this day and age. You should add that many words to your vocabulary each week. Many popular magazines publish features that will help you in this area.

And, finally, realize that graduating from school is just the beginning—the commencement—of your days and years of learning. And with wisdom will come kindness, patience, love, understanding, and success as a person. It's never too late to begin.

EXERCISES

1. Rate your knowledge of the English language. Is it "excellent," "good," "fair" or "poor"?

   _____

2. Set goals for improving your vocabulary and usage. (Include books to read, audio programs to listen to, courses to take, a number of new words to learn each week.)

   _____

   _____

   _____

   _____

   _____

   _____

   _____

   _____

   _____

   _____

   _____

   _____

   _____

   _____

   _____

   _____

   _____

3. Set goals for increasing your knowledge of your area of interest, for upgrading your job skills. (Include books and periodicals to read, audio programs to listen to, courses and seminars to attend.)

_____

_____

_____

_____

_____

_____

_____

_____

_____

_____

_____

_____

_____

_____

_____

11

TODAY'S GREATEST ADVENTURE

We've defined success as the progressive realization of a worthy goal. The purpose of this message is to tell you of a wonderful way to keep realizing—to keep achieving—your goals, one after another, in the years ahead.

A goal sometimes seems so far off, and our progress often appears to be so painfully slow, that we have a tendency to lose heart. It sometimes seems we'll never make the grade. And we come close to falling back into old habits that, while they may be comfortable now, lead to nowhere.

Well, there's a way to beat this. It's been used successfully by many of the world's most successful people, and it's been advocated by many of the greatest thinkers. It's to live successfully *one day at a time!*

A lifetime is comprised of days, strung together into weeks, months, and years. Let's reduce it to a single day, and then, still further, to each task of that day.

A successful life is nothing more than a lot of successful days put together. It's going to take so many days to reach your goal. If this goal is to be reached in a minimum amount of time, every day must count.

Think of a single day as a building block with which you're building the tower of your life. Just as a stonemason can put only one stone in place at a time, you can live only one day at a time. And it's the way in which these stones are placed that will determine the beauty and strength of your tower. If each stone is successfully placed, the tower will be a success. If, on the other hand, the stones are put down in a hit-or-miss fashion, the whole tower is in danger. Now, this may seem to be a rather elementary way of looking at it, but I want to make my point clear—and it's a good and logical way of looking at a human life.

All right, then, let's take it one day at a time, from the time we wake up in the morning until we drop off to sleep that night, keeping our goal in mind as often as possible.

Now, each day consists of a series of tasks—tasks of all kinds. And the success of a day depends upon the successful completion of most of these tasks. If everything we do during the day is a success—that is, done in the best fashion of which we're capable—we can fall asleep that night in the comfortable knowledge that we've done our very best, that our day has been a success, that one more stone has been successfully put into place.

This is the way to really live!

Do, each day, all that can be done that day. You don't need to overwork—or to rush blindly in to your work, trying to do the greatest possible number of things in the shortest possible amount of time. Don't try to do tomorrow's—or next week's—work today. It's not so much the number of things you do but the quality, the efficiency of each separate action that counts. Gradually, you'll find yourself increasing the number of tasks and performing them all much more efficiently.

To get the habit of success (and that's why successful people go from one success to another—because it's a habit with them), you need only to succeed in the small tasks of each day. This makes a successful day. With enough of these, you have a successful week, month, year—and lifetime.

This is why I say success is not a matter of luck—far from it. It can be predicted and guaranteed, and anyone can achieve it by following this plan. Almost before you realize it, you'll have achieved your goal. In looking back, you'll realize that your success was not attributable to any one day, week, or month. Rather, it was the consistent, unrelenting, successful succession of single days that did the trick. This is the way a skyscraper, a home, or a human life is successfully built. One successful day at a time; and each day comprising a collection of successful tasks—one successful task at a time.

To advance to the place you've chosen, two things are necessary: (1) that you keep your eye on your goal, and (2) that you continue to grow in competence and effectiveness.

Don't get impatient. Don't let hundreds of little distractions that, each day, try to get you off course bother you. Pay no attention to them. Shake them off, and stay steadily on the track. Concentrate on each task of the day, from morning to night, and do each as successfully as you can.

Know full well that if each of your tasks—or at least the great majority of them—is performed successfully, your life has to be successful. There's no other result. There's no way to avoid it.

The men and women who are certain to advance are the ones who become too big for their jobs, who have a clear concept of what they want to be, who know that they can become what they want to become, and who are determined to be what they want to be. Remind yourself at this time that people become exactly what they make up their minds to become.

Are you too big for your present job? If it's obvious to you that you are, it's obvious to others. People are not "given" promotions, as a rule. They promote themselves by becoming too big for their jobs, and by making up their minds exactly what bigger and better jobs, or incomes, they're shooting for. And this is done by taking one day at a time, one task at a time, during each day.

But how do we separate the important tasks from the unimportant ones? Did you ever hear about the single idea for which a man was paid $25,000? It was worth every penny of it!

The story goes that the president of a big steel company had granted an interview to an efficiency expert named Ivy Lee. Lee was telling his prospective client how he could help him do a better job of managing the company, when the president broke in to say something to the effect that he wasn't at present managing as well as he knew how. He went on to tell Ivy Lee that what was needed wasn't more knowing, but a lot more doing. He said, "We know what we should be doing. If you can show us a better way of getting it done, I'll listen to you—and pay you anything within reason you ask."

Lee then said that he could give him something in 20 minutes that would increase his efficiency by at least 50 percent. He then handed the executive a blank sheet of paper and said, "Write down on this paper the six most important things you have to do tomorrow." The executive thought about it and did as requested. It took him about three or four minutes.

Lee then said, "Now number them in the order of their importance to you and to the company." That took another, three, four, or five minutes.

Then Lee said, "Now put the paper in your pocket, and the first thing tomorrow morning, take it out and look at item number one. Don't look at the others, just number one, and start working on it. And if you can, stay with it until it's completed. Then take item number two the same way; then number three, and so on, until you have to quit for the day."

"Don't worry if you have finished only one or two items on your list. The others can wait. If you can't finish them all by this method, you couldn't have finished them with any other method. And without some system, you'd probably take 10 times as long to finish them—and might not even have them in the order of their importance."

"Do this every working day," Lee went on. "After you've convinced yourself of the value of this system, have your men try it. Try it as long as you like, and then send me your check for whatever you think the idea is worth."

The entire interview hadn't taken more than a half-hour. In a few weeks, the story has it, the company president sent Ivy Lee a check for $25,000, with a letter saying the lesson was the most profitable, from a money standpoint, he had ever learned in his life. And it is said that this plan was largely responsible for turning what was then a little-known steel company into one of the biggest independent steel producers in the world.

One idea! The idea of taking things one at a time, in their proper order; of staying with one task until it's successfully completed before going on to the next; of living one day at a time.

For the next seven days, try the $25,000 idea in your life. Tonight, write on a slip of paper the six most important things you have to do. Then number them in the order of their importance. Tomorrow morning, go to work on item number one, and stay with it until it's successfully completed. Then move on to number two, and so on. When you've finished with all six, get another piece of paper, and repeat the process.

You'll be astonished and delighted by the order this brings into your life—and by the rate of speed with which you'll be able to accomplish the things that need doing, in the order of their importance. This simple but tremendously effective method will take all the confusion out of your life. You'll never find yourself running around in circles, wondering what to do next.

As you use this method, remember to live the best you can, one day at a time. You need not worry about tomorrow, or the next day, or what's going to happen at the end of the month. One day at a time, handled successfully, will carry you over every hurdle; it will solve every problem. You can relax in the happy knowledge that successful tasks make successful days, which, in turn, build a successful life. This is the kind of unassailable logic no one can argue with. It will work every time—for every person.

The reason for writing down what you consider only the most important things to do is obvious. Handling each task during the day successfully is important to the degree of the importance of the task itself. Successfully doing a lot of unnecessary things can be pretty much a waste of time. Make certain that the tasks you take time to do efficiently are important tasks—tasks that move you ahead, steadily, toward your goal.

So often, youngsters in school worry about getting a passing grade. They think of all they'll have to do before the end of the school year. Following this course of action, they can stop worrying completely and count on excellent grades.

Freshmen in high school and college are frequently plagued by doubts as to whether they'll be able to successfully complete the four years ahead and graduate. Four years seem like such a long time to them—almost forever. And this thought sometimes leads to a sort of giving up—a fear of failure.

It was the great Harvard University teacher and psychologist, William James, who said, in effect, let not students worry about the success of their efforts. If they will do each day as best they can the work which is before them, they will wake up one day to find themselves among the competent people of their generation.

Student, junior executive, homemaker, senior executive, or professional—this plan works for everybody. It removes doubt, fear, and worry, and it brings order into our lives.

All any of us needs to do is face each day as it comes in good cheer, knowing that we have only to succeed today to guarantee our future. In this way, we'll move steadily ahead—growing more competent, more confident, with the passing of every day. Others may seem to suddenly shoot up faster . . . and operate in spurts and fits, but it is to the steady that the rewards are eventually paid.

Saint Edmund, archbishop of Canterbury, was right when he said, "Work as though you would live forever; but live as though you would die tomorrow."

Now try writing down the six most important things you have to do tomorrow. Then number them in the order of their importance. Really do this. First thing tomorrow morning, tackle item number one, and stay with it until it's completed. If something should force its delay, move on to number two. But take your tasks in order, and finish them in order as best you can. And try not to get sidetracked by people or things.

I have glued to the wall beside my typewriter a great saying by Ernest Hemingway. He said, "Write as well as you can, and finish what you start."

There's nothing mysterious, or capricious, about achieving outstanding success. It's completely within our individual control, and it's absolutely predictable. It's simply a matter of doing certain things in a certain way, every day. That's all there is to it—as long as you have that goal to work toward. There's no valid reason on earth why you should not become really successful in your field, your home life, and your community.

Remember that everything in the entire limitless universe operates according to the law of cause and effect. There are no exceptions to this. Nothing happens by accident. For every result, there's a cause. You have only to take care of the cause; the effect will always, without exception, take care of itself. Good cause; good effect. No cause; no effect. Bad cause; bad effect. It's as reliable as the rising of the sun.

This business of living the best we can one day at a time has an almost unbelievable cumulative effect for good—for success and for the things we want.

Sometimes when we see a bricklayer starting on a building and putting the first brick in place, we're struck by the size of the job he has ahead of him. But one day, almost before we realize it, he's finished. All the thousands of bricks are in place—each one vital to the finished structure, each one sharing its portion of the load. And so should be the days of a human life. And we'll be proud and happy with the finished product.

EXERCISES

1. Try the $25,000 idea in your life: Write on a sheet of paper the six most important things you have to do each day, Then number them in their order of importance. Work on item number one until it is successfully completed. Then move on to number two, and so on. When you've finished with all six, get another sheet of paper, and repeat the process.

2. Make certain that the tasks you spend your time on are important ones—tasks that will move you ahead, steadily, toward your goal.

   List below any tasks that you might be able to delegate to others or even eliminate from your agenda—tasks that, over time, have become unnecessary or obsolete.

   _____

   _____

   _____

   _____

   _____

   _____

   _____

   _____

   _____

   _____

   _____

   _____

3. How well do you deal with interruptions and distractions? If you are often sidetracked during your day—by nonurgent telephone calls, drop-in visitors, etc.—plan a strategy for handling those diversions.

_____

_____

_____

_____

_____

_____

_____

_____

_____

_____

_____

_____

12

THE PERSON ON THE
WHITE HORSE

All businesses, all organizations, from the smallest to the largest, need a leader. They have their committees, their echelons of command and, perhaps, a widely dispersed group of semiautonomous divisions; but the overall company, and each of its divisions, must have strong and able leadership.

Contrary to popular belief, you do not raise morale in an organization; it filters down from the top. The attitudes of the people working in any organization will always reflect the attitude of the leader. And this leader will always be found to be just one person: the man or woman on the white horse.

I'm sure you're aware that even the largest and oldest companies, with many thousands of employees and hundreds of management people, will, when they find themselves in trouble, or not doing as well as they should, seek out one person and place him in the position of final authority. The whole company, the board of directors, and, perhaps, thousands of stockholders all look to this one person for leadership and success. The case of Chrysler Corporation and Lee Iacocca is an excellent example.

Wherever you find a successful, going concern—whether it's a gas station, a supermarket, a school club, a PTA, or a well-organized home—you'll find behind its success an outstanding leader. This is the most valuable person in society. In industry, he makes the wheels turn—the entire economy work. This is the person who's responsible for the growth of nations and their position in the world; he's the employer of millions; he's the dreamer, the planner. To him, a clock is something that other people watch. You'll find this person working early and late, and when he's not working, he's usually thinking and planning.

Way back during the depression of the 1930s, the refrain most often heard by employers was, "I'll do anything. Just give me a job." Millions were unemployed; thousands of business firms had closed their doors; and outside employment offices, long lines of people stood waiting for any kind of work.

It was during this time, in Long Beach, California, which was crowded to overflowing with thousands who had migrated there looking for work (when there wasn't enough work to go around for the permanent residents, it seemed), that a friend of mine made an interesting discovery: He found that he could go to work almost anywhere he chose. Now, as amazing as this may sound, it is absolutely true!

One day, it dawned upon him that the business establishments of various kinds were just as anxious to succeed as were the people looking for work.

The owners and managers of these businesses were worried about the hard times that had descended upon the country, and a great many of them were looking for someone to come to their aid— the person who would somehow show up and solve their business problems. But all they heard was people asking for work, saying, "I'll do anything." These people were asking for a paycheck from a company that was very likely teetering on the brink of financial ruin itself. So in windows of businesses all over the land, signs appeared, reading, "No Help Wanted." This was a form of negative advertising, and while it kept the plaintive hordes away from the door, it also hurt business.

Well, my friend decided to become part of the solution, instead of a part of the problem. His method was simple, and it worked like a charm. He selected the kind of business he felt he would like to work in, and in which he could build a career. He then devoted a month to finding out all he could about that particular business. He talked to other people in the same line; he heard their problems, and what they felt was wrong. He talked for hours, probing, asking questions about what they felt was needed, and so on. He went to the public library and read everything he could find on that industry. Then he began to think of ways and means by which this business might be improved.

When he was ready, and finally made his call on the company for which he had decided to work, instead of asking for a job, he said

176 • LEAD THE FIELD

to the boss something like this: "I believe I know of several ways in which your business can be greatly increased, and I'd like to talk to you about them."

Here he was, selling the one thing on earth in which his prospect was most interested. The fact that he now knew a good deal about the business permitted him to talk intelligently. He took a positive attitude, he expressed a willingness to pitch in and help to put the business on a sound and profitable footing, and, of course—that's right—he got the job. Millions were out of work and asking for jobs, but one man found a way to be of help.

What had he done? Well, first, he had specialized; he had selected one line of work and decided that was where his future would be. Then he had to prove himself, and he did.

The "jack-of-all-trades and master of none" was the person who suffered during the Depression. People who knew what they were doing and where they were going sailed through those Depression years, just as a large ship sails through a storm. It wasn't as comfortable as it could have been, but at least the crossing was a success—at least they didn't founder.

And thousands of businesses actually grew larger and prospered during the Depression.

The best way for you to develop the security that lasts a lifetime is to become outstanding at one particular line of work. Look at it this way: Regardless of economic ups and downs, the industry of which that line of work is a part will continue to operate. It won't shut down completely. As long as you're in the top 5 percent of the people in that industry, you know you'll always be in demand—you'll be wanted and needed in that industry. . . .

The man or woman who becomes truly outstanding at what he or she does has the world on a string. Here's the person of confidence and peace of mind. Here's the person who is quietly aware of his or her ability and has an intimate knowledge of his or her job and industry. Here's the homemaker or student who is at the top of the group. This person has it made, and he or she, and everybody else, knows it.

Ask yourself this question: "Am I now such a person?" Down deep inside, you know the answer. If you answered yes, you're among the most fortunate people—and in one of the smallest and most select groups on earth. If your answer was no, it can be turned into a yes in a surprisingly short time.

The first step is to make one really big and important decision. It's a decision the great majority of people never make, and they suffer as a result. Failing to make this decision keeps a person from ever really getting on course or clarifying his goals. If you'll make the decision I'm recommending, you can take a deep breath, give a comfortable sigh of relief, fix your eyes firmly upon your target, and go to work relaxed, comfortable, and sure in the knowledge that the success you seek will be yours.

When he was asked the formula for success, the great steel magnate, Andrew Carnegie, answered, "Put all your eggs in one basket, and then watch the basket."

Let's be frankly realistic. Who gets laid off work during an economic slump? Well, what gets thrown over the side when a ship is in danger of going down? Everything not absolutely essential to the operation of the vessel and the safety of her passengers. And it's the same in a business or any other organization. It has to be that way.

A corporation's main purpose is to remain in business forever. As long as it remains in business, it can provide a needed product or service, protect the investment of those who have faith in it, and provide jobs for those who are essential to its continuity of operation. It's the duty of management to protect the firm and the people who depend upon it, just as it's the captain's duty to do everything in his power to keep his ship sailing.

All a person needs to do is make certain that he is a vital part of the business or organization. Those who insist on remaining spare gear, those who do no more than they must in order to squeak by—those who say, "I'm not going to do any more than I'm paid to do"—must expect to be jettisoned when things get too rough for safety.

Nobody, particularly the captain, likes to see cargo thrown over the side, but if it will help save the ship, there's nothing else he can do.

That's why people are laid off. It has nothing to do with management and labor relations, or personalities. And in the long run, it's best for everyone, since once smooth sailing has again been reached, additional employment can again be made available. So each of us must decide whether he wants to be a part of the cargo or a member of the crew.

It's said that millions suffer today from a malady called panaphobia. Panaphobia means, literally, "fear of everything." It's an uneasy feeling, a feeling of insecurity, that generally manifests itself as a sort of lump of fear that settles right behind the belt buckle—especially on Sunday evenings and on Monday mornings. . . . It's an apprehension, a feeling of foreboding.

This extremely unpleasant condition is said to result from the unspoken but realized fact that we're getting credit for more than we're actually doing, or that we're doing less that we could be doing. It's the perfectly natural and normal understanding deep within us that there's something basically wrong about getting praise that's not earned or, if we are employees, being paid for something we're not doing as well as we possibly can.

If we have panaphobia, running does no good. We find it follows us on vacation, and around the house and yard on weekends. It's inside us, and no matter how fast the jet we board, or how exciting the television program we watch, soon we're aware of it again.

There's a simple cure for this malady. It's to throw ourselves not out of a window, but into activity, into our work. It's the decision to be worth more than we're being paid. Only in this way can we grow. It's overbalancing the scales in the service we give, knowing that our rewards must follow as a natural result.

Anyone who is honest with himself realizes that he has been happiest and most satisfied after having successfully completed a difficult job.

A leader is a person who can help and lead others. It's the conscientious mother who wants her children to grow up knowing the rules for success and happiness. It's the father who shows by example that any job worth doing is worth doing well. It's the student who studies to learn, not just to get a grade—who has a mind of his own and sets the pace for his fellow students. It's the farmer whose farm sets an example in his area. It's the businessperson whose small business continues to grow and prosper with the passing years. It's the employee who has the good sense to realize that one gets most out of any job by giving loyalty and dedication to the firm that pays his wages. A leader is any person who realizes the importance of becoming a bigger and better person with the passing of every day, week, and month. A leader takes the responsibility for his own growth; he's a planner, a thinker, a doer.

Each of us can become such a leader in his own area of activity. It's not difficult. And in the long run, it's easier for us, and on us, than what at first may appear to be the easier of two courses.

Simply fix your eyes upon your goal—visualize it with every ounce of your being; enjoy the prospect of it—and courageously set out toward it. Maintain a cheerful, helpful attitude toward everyone. Why shouldn't you be cheerful, since you know you'll achieve everything you've set your heart upon?

Become a sponge for information that will help you on your way. You don't have to waste years making the mistakes others have made before.

You'll be surprised at how quickly you'll reach your goal. But don't be impatient. Know and have faith that what should come to you will come to you at the right time. Everything in the world works on the side of the person who works with nature's laws.

And, above all—if you should forget everything else—remember that everything about you—everything you will ever have, know, experience in any way—operates in accordance with law, law that is true and unchanging, the law of the stars and of the balance of the world.

As Emerson wrote: "Let him learn a prudence of a higher strain. Let him learn that everything in nature, even dust and feathers, goes by law and not by luck . . . and that what he sows, he reaps!"

Look about you; take stock of your present situation, because it's nothing more or less than the result of your past sowing. Are you happy with it? Is it what you want? Then you know what you must sow—today and tomorrow and the next day. And in the sowing, rest in the calm, serene, and cheerful certainty that, having sown, you will then reap, all the years of your life, the rich results that come automatically—the abundant harvest.

Now, this is Earl Nightingale reminding you that success as a human being in modern society does not come naturally. It requires the conscious utilization of ourselves in the service of others. We have our minds, our genetic possibilities, a certain amount of time, and our free will. We belong to the world minority that lives in a free society. We become whatever we seriously make up our minds to become. That's possible because whatever we seriously decide to do is naturally linked to our genetic possibilities. A person with little or no aptitude for science will never decide to become a scientist. A naturally shy and retiring person will never take a job in sales, or, if he does, he will soon get out of it.

Each of us has his own inner voice. Emerson referred to it as that "iron string" that vibrates within us.

Each of us wants to succeed during his holiday on earth, and each of us should. But we don't succeed in groups; we succeed or fail as individuals.

In *Lead the Field* you have read the best basic information and the great ideas we need to reach whatever goal we seriously choose.

Reread this book often. You will be astonished to discover how much you missed during your first and second readings. Each time we read, different ideas will catch our interest or more deeply engage our imagination or strengthen our resolve to put them into practice.

Think of this book and the other Nightingale-Conant resources as your partners in success. You can always refer back to them. You'll find yourself delighted by the new enthusiasm and excitement you'll experience as you bring new meaning and new rewards into your life.

Thank you.

EXERCISES

1. Evaluate your leadership skills, and note any ideas for improvement below:

_____

_____

_____

_____

_____

_____

_____

_____

_____

_____

_____

_____

_____

_____

_____

_____

_____

_____

2. How can you develop what Earl Nightingale calls "the security that lasts a lifetime"?

_____

_____

_____

_____

_____

_____

_____

_____

_____

_____

_____

_____

_____

_____

_____

_____

_____

_____

3. Resolve to, each day, do more than you are paid to do.

NOTES

For more information about additional
Earl Nightingale's classic books check out
www.soundwisdom.com

To purchase Earl Nightingale's audiobooks
go to www.nightingale.com